Endorsements

"I love this book! I am passionate about good health and marriage to my highway patrolman. *A CHiP on my Shoulder* speaks to both, making choices for a healthy law enforcement marriage. Victoria speaks candidly of the challenges unique to cops and their relationships, and offers positive ways to handle them." - **Alison Sweeney, Actress and Wife of a California Highway Patrolman**

"A wonderful, life saving, life affirming book! Required reading for every cop, and for every cop's spouse, and for all those who love and support our cops." - **Lt. Col. Dave Grossman, USA (ret.), Author of *On Combat* and *On Killing***

"Victoria's book provides viable strategies, relevant and timely information, as well as practical advice, making this book a powerful antidote to the corrosive affect a career in law enforcement can have on a marriage." - **Barbara Upham, OEA Sergeant-Retired, California Highway Patrol**

"In her book, *A CHiP on my Shoulder*, Victoria Newman offers a career of practical advice for the emergency responder spouse/partner. The goal of presenting real life issues paired with straightforward thinking and problem solving is reached many times throughout the book." - **Joel Fay, PsyD, President of West Coast Post-Trauma Retreat**

"A CHiP on my Shoulder is realistic, positive and filled with simple wisdom. Victoria's candid account of life married to a California Highway Patrolman covers a lot of ground. Reading it is like talking with a trusted friend." - **Ellen Kirschman, PhD, Author of *I Love a Cop: What Police Families Need to Know***

"The foundation of every ethical, competent law enforcement officer is a solid personal life. *A CHiP on my Shoulder* is a survival guide for the police family that functions as a road map to keep that police family solid. The law enforcement landscape tragically is filled with failed marriages and broken families that could have been avoided. Victoria points out how to not become one of those statistics. She shows us that a successful police marriage is not based on whether the two people loved each other at the starting point of their life together, but rather how they live out that love each day. *A CHiP on my Shoulder* gives law enforcement specific insights into the journey. It should be given to the significant others of all police academy graduates as part of their survival training." - **Kevin M. Gilmartin, PhD, Author of *Emotional Survival for Law Enforcement: A Guide for Officers and Their Families***

"Life in a law enforcement marriage is sometimes frustrating, sometimes frightening, sometimes a roller coaster thrill ride and often a rewarding personal journey. *A CHiP on my Shoulder* is a warm and insightful glimpse into the challenge of keeping the "shine" on a law enforcement relationship. With tenderness and good humor, Victoria delivers sound advice and words of wisdom that are sure to benefit families of law enforcement personnel, whether they are green-at-the-gills rookies or old-timers trying to figure out 'what happened here?!' A read of this book is a great investment in your law enforcement relationship bank account." - **Elizabeth Dansie, M.A., B.C.E.T.S., The Psychological Services Group**

What Readers Say

"What an awesome book for wives of law enforcement, military, and first responders." Rachel, CA

"A refreshing resource in an arid field of need." Jim, AR

"My husband and I have had hard times...on a night it seemed like everything came to a head, I picked up your book and read about your experience on the beach...it was exactly what I needed at that moment. I shared it with my husband and it got him to finally agree to counseling... you really saved me when I needed it most." Amanda, CA

"So much of what you wrote about I could totally relate to as 'the mom'!" Cindy, CA

"This book has something everyone can learn and love." Amy, WV

"Sometimes we just need someone to say, 'Hey, you can do this.'" Lynn, CA

"I just LOVE your book. My LEO is reading it as well and it is so amazing how much it is bringing us together for great conversation to better our relationship." Katie, WI

"My husband is retired Air Force...I thought it could be written for the military wives also. I will read it again!" Connie, IA

"Easy flowing and picture words that say so much." Diane, CA

"The more I read on being a cop's wife the more I understand, the better wife I know I can be for him. We've struggled with a lot of the things you mention in the book, and I wish I had started reading about this life long before I did." Sara, ME

"This book opened my eyes and my heart and is a much needed read for good or struggling marriages. Felt at times I was writing parts of it!" Lisa, CA

"I read the entire book in two hours...it hit so close to home." Christine, IL

"It validated so many of my feelings and made me look at things in a different light." Courtney

"I finished your book on the plane home...while I was gone one of our local police officers was killed in the line of duty. My husband was present on scene. The chapter on tragedy was incredibly informative and helpful." Karen, MI

"THE resource to go to...easy to read, practical, down-to-earth." Jim, TN

"It's very reassuring to see myself in many of the situations you mention." Samantha, CA

"Required reading for every LEOW and fiancé in the United States. This work will bless many people and many marriages." Dale, GA

"It was as if you wrote the book for me!" Nicole, CA

A Chip on my Shoulder

A CHIP ON MY SHOULDER

HOW TO LOVE AND SUPPORT YOUR COP

Victoria M. Newman
Third Edition

Published in the United States of America

ISBN-13: 9781542753111
ISBN-10: 1542753112

Photography by Donna Shelby Photography
Cover Design by Dave Eaton Creative

Library of Congress Control Number: 2017913227
CreateSpace Independent Publishing Platform
North Charleston, South Carolina

DEDICATION

For the CHiP on my shoulder. Whatever life holds for us, I'm glad we'll be holding each other.
I love you, Brent.

TABLE OF CONTENTS

Preface

In 2010, I set out to write my story as a police wife. I invited some wives over, fed them dinner, and listened. I also interviewed police wives I came into contact with, and found themes that resonated. *A CHiP on my Shoulder—How to Love Your Cop with Attitude* was written, published and released in September 2011.

The response has been amazing. Letters, meeting precious police family members, walking through life together, and deep connections ensued. The critics were there, of course, but most police wives said *CHiP* was *their* story. Traveling the country began shortly thereafter (and a couple other countries, too). I was able to meet many police families, talk face-to-face, and hug a lot of hurting people. Listening to the stories and what others have experienced gave me an even deeper understanding of what this life is about.

In 2014, the Michael Brown/Darren Wilson incident in Ferguson, Missouri awakened a deep anger, and people took to the streets. We'd seen that before, especially here in California, but something was different. It ignited a flame of hate and rage—and a campaign of anti-police rhetoric spread like wildfire through communities via avenues of social media.

It changed things for police officers and their families. Harassment. Home addresses published. Murderous chants in the streets and on Facebook. It's been pretty tough. Soon the guns were blazing, and law enforcement families across the country were splintered, grief-stricken, and fearful. Though its intensity ebbs and flows, it's made being a police family all the more difficult.

After my original publisher abruptly closed their doors in 2017, I decided to rewrite *CHiP*, adding more tools, addressing the challenges we face post-Ferguson, and incorporating the wisdom and stories I've collected since 2010. What you hold in your hands is the result. Some content is the same, some has been updated, and much is new.

My husband has served with the California Highway Patrol for almost 30 years. The title is attributed to him, as here in California we sometimes refer to our officers as CHiPs (after the TV show from the 70s). However, this book was written for *all* law enforcement wives. I share candidly about our marriage, but the tales told are not exclusively real stories of the highway patrol. Stories and perspectives were gleaned from all over the United States and Canada.

Law enforcement families have a lot of faces. I chose to write this book from my own personal point of view as a woman married to a male officer. This is not meant to exclude those who have a different situation. More than 10 percent of law enforcement officers are women, and there are many non-traditional relationships that make up our law enforcement community. The principles and ideas presented here are beneficial for any long-term relationship.

Lastly, this book is written specifically for the spouse of a law enforce-ment officer. But every marriage takes two people! For this reason, I wrote *A Marriage in Progress—Tactical Support for Law Enforcement Relationships*. These two books go together. Extended family members have benefitted from the information in that book as well.

My hope is that the thoughts shared within these pages will encour-age you, giving you tools for your toolbox, and empower your marriage to what it can be. Many spouses have told me their officers have read it as well, and it has brought about some great conversations. Also included are discussion group questions at the end of each chapter in the event that you read through the book with others. It could be the start of some new friendships as you come alongside each other and talk through the issues you share as law enforcement families. As we move forward since Ferguson, it is more important than ever to be united as couples. Our support at home is more important than ever, as is the support we receive for ourselves.

If you want more information or further contact with me, please visit my website: www.how2loveyourcop.com. You will find even more information and resources that specifically apply to your family.

God Bless You!

Victoria

ACKNOWLEDGEMENTS

Although there is only one name on the cover, many aspects of this book were put together by a team who adopted my vision and joined my effort in several capacities. I give credit to the following:

My readers: Ginny Yttrup; Teddi Depner; Beth Dansie; Barb Upham; Joel Fay; Michelle Walker; Ellen Kirschman; Mindi Russell; Kevin Gilmartin; Rebecca Qualls; Bernie Homme; Dave Grossman; and my husband, Brent. Each read parts of the manuscript, providing valuable feedback. I appreciate the time and critique they provided. It was exactly what this book needed. Many thanks.

My focus group members (last names withheld to protect their privacy): Kim, Julie, Beth, Stephanie, Maria, Susan, Diana, Erin, Frances, Tricia, Rebecca, Christina, Debbie, Bonnie, Candy, Wendy, and Sandy provided stories, quotes, and input. I also interviewed several others individually and have added their stories as well: Rodney; Clarke; Lori; Emmett; Rachel; Tracy; James; Anna; Barb; Rachel; Chris; and my grandparents, Bernie and Helen. Their support and willingness to speak candidly proved invaluable in my writing and will be a blessing to those who read this book.

My writer's group—Linda, Barb, Ginny, Tammy, Dee, Rebecca, and Teddi—have allowed me to share my dream and bounce ideas off them for several years now. My thanks to them for journeying with me through tears and laughter.

My support team—Rachel; Mike and Nancy; David and Amanda; Donna; Christina; Rachel; Nancy; Jill; Renee; Kathryn; Kathryn; Lorie;

Linda; Rachel; Rebecca; Deb; Barb; Janice; Gary and Mary; Bernie and Helen; Rose; Paula; Annette; Mary; Tammie; Jenny; Sharol; Brent; Dee; Ginny; Bonnie; Fred; Carol; Kris; Barbara and Frances—prayed and encouraged me for months. Thanks to them for many notes, calls, and prayers. They've been my strength and perseverance.

There are several others who put in time to help me when needed. Donna Shelby and Russell and Kira Stevens spent a full (but fun) day contributing to the amazing cover. Kathryn Redman offered excellent marketing direction. Dave and Rose Wertheim lent direction and experience. Barb Upham, Omar Watson and Bernie Homme assisted with my endorsements. And countless others have offered support, ideas and kind words throughout this journey. May God bless you!

My kids—Kyrie, Ben, Annika, and David—have been on this journey with me day by day. They cooked and cleaned, solved problems on their own, and gave me permission to hide out in the office for hours. They listened with interest and provided feedback with hugs and encouragement. They dried my tears and celebrated with me with enthusiasm and love. I appreciate each one of them.

Brent has been incredibly supportive through each step of this entire journey, and I am so thankful for him. He has been willing to speak truth into my life, to be vulnerable on the pages for the sake of other marriages, to offer wisdom in several conversations, and has told many others about the book. I couldn't have done this without him.

Everything I am and will be I owe to Jesus Christ. I thank Him for the call and thank Him for my dream. He will keep leading me, loving me, and changing me. All the credit goes to Him.

Many thanks to each and every one of you!

FOREWORD

As a career Law Enforcement Chaplain for over 25 years, too often I have seen the destruction of marriages between officers and their spouses. Many times our law enforcement couples enter this career with an altruistic view of the profession and believe it is a *call* on their lives. Marriage is *tough*. Relationships take *work*. Now, add the distinctive culture of the law enforcement profession and it becomes *tough work*. Law enforcement couples are simply not aware of the demands nor the sacrifices put on their marriage and relationship. I believe this book can be the beginning of renewal for couples. Victoria puts things in perspective. Her personal observations and practical strategies come from her marriage to a law enforcement husband. Victoria helps officers and their spouses that are struggling with the issues of this profession.

As I read *A CHIP on my Shoulder*, two issues were very apparent. First, Victoria has defined the uniqueness of the law enforcement culture. She has shown what it takes to serve and, in turn, what is taken (emotionally, spiritually, physically, and mentally) from these highly committed men and women. They *are* the line between civility and anarchy. She explains the powers and decision-making that no other occupation has: the ability to take away an individual's unalienable rights (life, liberty, and the pursuit of happiness). With just cause, the officer has a profound effect on individual lives, howbeit, settling disputes, investigating accidents and crimes, arresting offenders, testifying in court, aiding the sick, injured, abused, and disturbed, and dealing with all kinds of death.

While 96% of law enforcement academies teach officer safety and how to deal with these problems, they don't spend near enough time on *being human,* or in other words, emotional safety. With all of broken humanity, how could they not be affected by the evil they feel, see, hear, touch and smell? How could this pain not transfer to the humanness of our officers? How could this not be a daily assault on their marriages, their well-being, and their perceptions of society?

Secondly, Victoria reveals a truth as a wife: that the best person who can and should stand in the gap for the officer is the spouse. "And the two shall become as one" reminds us that we have to keep both parts healthy. She further explains that the spouse must be just as committed to the *call* as the officer is. Victoria addresses boundaries and expectations of what is normal in this abnormal 24-hour profession. She explains that law enforcement marriages can survive this career and be healthy and happy as well.

For officers who read this book, my prayer is that your emotions will be calmed and your heart will be reminded that you took an oath of commitment and determination to be the best warrior for justice and champion for the innocent you could be. All the sweat and tears in the academy's training paid off. You made it. Great! For officers and spouses, the oath you took as a couple needs that same commitment and determination to prepare for a productive life together.

Read *A CHiP on my Shoulder.* It could be the difference between life and death in your marriage.

Reverend Master Senior Chaplain Mindi Russell, Sacramento County, California

Introduction

"Marriage is hard," he warned. "Marriage to a cop is even harder. You need to think through if you truly want to do this. Do you think you have what it takes to be the few who make it? Most cops are divorced..." The background investigator could tell I wasn't fazed. Which is why he repeated it.

I thought, *How hard could it be? I love him, he loves me. Of course we would make it work.* I didn't really listen because my thoughts were on flowers and white lacy dresses and invitations to our wedding. I thought he was being overly dramatic. I thought he was unnecessarily negative. I wasn't ready to hear how difficult it would be as we embarked on this journey.

So months later, when I found myself in the heart of Los Angeles traffic, scared to death to make a lane change, I remembered his words. I recounted them again when I heard the first heartbreaking stories of people who had taken or ruined lives. They echoed with the sound of a brush hitting the wall during an argument before Brent reported for duty on our first Christmas together. And I remembered his words as I sat on the bed, watching him prepare to enter the LA riots war zone. Slowly but surely, I got an inkling of what Officer Negative was talking about.

I've had a CHiP on my shoulder for almost three decades now. We've had a wild and crazy adventure with twists and turns and some seasons I don't care to repeat. Twelve moves, five promotions, and four kids later, I love him more now than in those early days. But that love didn't grow without choosing my attitudes carefully. I'd say this is the key to the success of our marriage and the heart of this book. I consciously make the effort to deal honestly with problems, adopt attitudes that don't come naturally, and am learning to set realistic expectations. It has been tough, but I am learning to be stronger than the circumstances. So can you.

Along our journey we've been involved in the lives of dozens of cops and their families. I've listened to officers and their spouses in their struggles with their marriages. Brent and I have mentored several couples together, and we've also met one-on-one. We've seen marriages on the brink of disaster come back to life through choices to forgive, moving forward, and incorporating changes needed to help their relationships survive. I've incorporated many of these stories here with their permission. In these cases their names have been changed to protect their privacy.

It takes a strong person to be a cop's life partner. We come in all different sizes, shapes, backgrounds, and experiences, but we have a common strength. This strength is determined by our hearts and minds. My goal is that these ideas and principles will be applied to individual marriages in unique and creative ways. My hope is that these pages will enrich your marriage, helping it to thrive for years to come.

I know a little bit about law enforcement because my father was a police officer. I'd watch him put on his uniform every day. I remember it very well. As a matter of fact, he made me shine his belt buckle and polish his shoes every morning. That part I hated, I have to admit it. But I loved watching him put on his uniform... He always let me put on his jacket first before he put it on. I remember I was so little the jacket went all the way down to the floor... And I watched him put his shield on his chest and walk proudly out of the door. That gave me the deep respect for our law enforcement officers and also for their families... Because I understand what it's like to say goodbye to your loved one each and every day and wonder if this is the day that they do not come home. Is this the day that there will be a knock on the door and our lives would change forever?

ARNOLD SCHWARZENEGGER
FORMER GOVERNOR OF CALIFORNIA
COMMENCEMENT ADDRESS AT THE CALIFORNIA HIGHWAY PATROL ACADEMY
JULY 9, 2010

CHAPTER 1
MR. AND MRS. COP: WHAT MAKES US DIFFERENT

*I actually am careful about what I wear to bed
when he's on duty. Because I never know when
another uniform will knock on my door...*
FRANCES, CALIFORNIA

*Life with an officer is never dull, predictable or planned.
Embrace the lifestyle, let go of the little things, and
always remember to make time for each other.*
MELINA, CALIFORNIA

I didn't sign up for this when I fell in love with my man. Brent was in that place of college indecision when we met. He had just realized that his first choice, the Air Force Academy, was not to be. There was a whole world of opportunity just waiting to be explored! So he looked into medicine and law, and he even considered becoming a pastor. Another choice was the California Highway Patrol. His dad was on the patrol and encouraged him to throw in an application. While we spent time getting to know each other, he was also following up on each step of the hiring process.

Then we got engaged. The first decision we made as a couple was to say yes to the patrol. We set our wedding date five weeks before he was to report to the California Highway Patrol Academy. I had no idea what I was in for. But I had my guy, and that was all that mattered.

In our minds, we committed to the patrol for five years. It was a way for us to grow up, get some life experience for medicine or ministry. But somewhere along the way, we let go of other opportunities. His career had become a calling.

He became a cop.

If you knew your husband before he became an officer, you probably witnessed a change in him. Maybe you met your man afterward and you knew what you were in for from the beginning. But, either way, we became law enforcement spouses and entered into a life that is different than non-cop spouses. Because he is in law enforcement, your marriage is different from others. But why?

Who He Is

Every society needs individuals who will step in and uphold the laws that the collective people agreed were necessary for peace. There will always be those who don't want to follow these rules. Some will, at times, go to significant effort to make sure they get their way and then get away with it. Our officers devote themselves to restoring and keeping the peace these people disrupt. We call it the thin blue line—the force that stands between order and chaos.

It's a tough position. Because our officers are protectors of the peace, they have to be on guard at all times in, and sometimes out, of uniform. Their safety is of utmost importance, as is the safety of their loved ones. As a precaution, protections can be put in place to minimize access to themselves and their families.

Protection of Privacy

When Brent and I moved to Los Angeles, we began to pay a small fee every month to keep our names out of the phonebook. Because I grew up in a small town, this was very foreign to me! But it was for our protection. My husband dealt with questionable characters on duty; therefore, payback was a possibility. One of the protections we put in place was controlling what information was available to the public. This was before the dawn of the Internet.

There are other things we do as well. We don't shout to the world what his occupation is. When we are out and about, we blend in. We keep to ourselves, but Brent is always watching. He sits in strategic spots with his back against a wall, in view of the exits. He will zero in on suspicious behavior and be ready to jump in (or leave), should something go awry. Most of the time, the kids and I aren't even aware of his vigilance.

We choose our friends wisely. Most cops end up hanging out with other cops, mainly because they understand and trust each other. Brent and I have maintained friendships with both cops and non-cops; it seems to keep our lives in balance. We haven't had any issues with this—most of the time. At times his cop mentality has offended others, but, for the most part, non-cop people are fascinated by the stories and ask lots of questions.

Neighbors are a different thing. We can't dictate who lives next door. Depending on the neighborhood, we've both kept quiet, and informed our neighbors that he was law enforcement. At times it has helped others to know who he is, but not everyone is happy about it.

One December night Brent was on the roof, putting up Christmas lights. Suddenly our neighbor pulled up and said that there was a young man dressed in dark clothing on the side of a single lady's home down the street. Brent jumped in the car and went to investigate, finding him hiding in a ravine. He instantly slipped into cop mode, interrogating the kid as to what he was doing. After an hour or so of following the kid home, calling the sheriff, and calming the neighbors' nerves, we went to bed. The next morning we awoke to vandalized Christmas decorations. Of course, we knew exactly who did it. The kid lived in a rental the next street over, so we held a neighborhood watch meeting, contacted the owner, and by Christmas they were gone. Wouldn't you know? A string of petty thefts in the area ended at the exact same time.

Stress

Perhaps the biggest impact on your marriage will be the stress of your officer's job. There are so many pressures on the police. There's the hatred from criminals, office politics, accusations from the media, a lack of justice in the court systems, armchair second-guessing, the heartbreaking deaths and crimes against innocent people, and even uneasiness of law-abiding citizens. It will, at times, affect him in his off time.

Your officer also undergoes physical stress. Not only does he need to rely on his training to get him out of some tight spots, but he also is required to work different shifts that aren't conducive to good sleep. On top of that, he may have trouble eating well, as many times they buy fat-laden fast food to sustain them during long hours (we've heard the donut jokes ad nauseum). And of course Monsters and Red Bull have become another food group. Our officers can also be susceptible to injuries or illnesses related to the job, and, of course, this will affect you.

Lastly, there are strong emotions that come with his job. He's been trained to be in control, to bring calm to stormy situations. Most will obey his orders, and the ones who don't may only respond to force. Sometimes it's hard to turn that off when he gets home. What if you and the kids don't adhere to something he wants or asks you to do? When your cop has strong emotions, both in control and out of control, they can affect your relationship and home.

Shift Work/Surveillance

Perhaps one of the most obvious things that set us apart from other marriages is the hours our officers work. Their jobs are driven by emergencies, and we never know what will happen and when. No matter what agency he works for, the hours can be long and unpredictable. Crime and accidents happen 24-7.

Brenna's husband, Scott, is on the SWAT team for the sheriff's department. He constantly gets calls to report for potential situations. At the onset of one recent incident, he kissed his family goodbye, saying he'd probably be home within the hour. It became a three-day hostage showdown. Scott came home a couple times to get some sleep and then returned. For Brenna and her children, it was the most difficult ordeal they'd experienced thus far. Their lives revolved around *the situation*. Family and friends called constantly for updates, Scott was in high gear the entire time, and it was covered in full-color detail on television.

In addition to long hours, in recent history we have endured something else—deployment. Natural disasters, 9/11, protests and riots, and fires have taken our officers to other places to help out local law enforcement in crisis situations. Many policemen are former military, so some spouses have experience with this. It doesn't make it any easier—and the spouse is left to hold down the fort.

Risk

I remember the news footage from September 11, 2001, as terrorists hijacked planes and crashed them into the Trade Towers. There were people of all shapes, sizes, ages, and colors fleeing a wall of dusty debris, leaving shoes, purses, and hats behind. My stomach tightened when I realized what happened. I thought about all the emergency personnel who were in the thick of where that debris was coming from. We lost many good men and women that day.

September 11 serves as a vivid reminder that what our officers do is dangerous. When everyone else is running *from* danger, they run *to* it. And we know full well the risk that they may not be the same when they return, if they return.

Over the years I've been to my share of law enforcement funerals. I've had widows and family members cry on my shoulder. We have a fallen officer who is buried within a mile of our home, and we visit his grave every year around Thanksgiving, the time of year he died. The risks are real. And the fear that this could happen to us can wreak havoc if not dealt with.

Emotional Effects

I once received a letter from a gal whose fiancé was going into police work. She asked, "How can he be unchanged by being a policeman? I don't want him to be phased by this life. Please tell me how to get him through it without changing him!" Unfortunately I had to gently tell her that there's no way around it. When a person deals with the sights, smells, and attitudes of the streets on a regular basis, he has to develop thick skin, or he won't make it. Our officers interact with mad, bad, and sad people every shift, and see the public at their worst. They are there in the most heartbreaking circumstances. They can't trust anyone—even in *routine* calls, if there is such a thing. This is for their safety. Brent's demeanor changed once he'd been on the job for awhile. What he saw, smelled, touched, and experienced found its way into his soul. I've talked with many officers and spouses that have been affected emotionally by incidents, or by an accumulation of different calls over time.

If you've been married to a cop for very long, I'm not telling you anything new. You've already come up with coping mechanisms and solutions to most of these issues. Sometimes all we need is to know that there are others who are experiencing the same thing, and we are bonded through the experience. But whatever stage you are in, dealing with these obstacles begins and ends in your mind.

A Battle for Your Mind

It was a beautiful morning but hot. A small group of men sat in chairs, facing us from the front, their duty uniforms blending in with the helicopters parked behind them. We were honored to be in their presence as the master of ceremonies recounted the heroics of these men while deployed in Afghanistan. Their ordeal sounded like a scene in a movie, but what they'd been through was very real. After they were awarded their distinguished medals, the families joined them up front for pictures. The officer we were there to support was joined only by his kids, as he was divorced.

I felt a lump in my throat. This brave yet humble man before us had been deployed twice to provide medical assistance to those fighting for our freedoms. When at home he serves as a police officer. I'm sure it was very difficult for his wife to endure the loneliness, the risks, and other things that make marriage to a soldier/cop challenging.

Being the spouse of a policeman, agent, deputy, or soldier is tough, and there are those who don't make it. I'd like to tell you it's not that difficult, but the facts speak for themselves. Divorce is a very real problem for law enforcement. But it isn't inevitable. Ellen Kirschman, PhD, a clinical psychologist who works with law enforcement and author of I Love a Cop, says this: "Several police-specific studies suggest that the first three years of marriage are the most precarious and that if a male officer stays married beyond those three years, his marriage is, in fact, more stable than one in the general population."[1]

---

1 Ellen Kirschman, I Love a Cop (New York: The Guilford Press, 2007) Page 5.

Sherry agrees with this. The third year of her marriage to her police officer was very difficult. Her husband couldn't juggle the new demands of his job, and they had been struggling for a couple of years. Both sides of their extended family were not familiar with the difficulties facing them as a new law enforcement couple and therefore didn't understand. Finally Sherry moved out. It got everyone's attention. Their relatives rallied around them, and after six months of processing and healing, they reunited. They are now enjoying a thriving marriage of eleven years.

Making the choice to stay or leave starts in the mind. When things are tough, there is a natural tendency to run. When hard times stay for a particularly long season, some women reach their breaking point. They need relief. And there are those who seek relief in leaving. But in many circumstances, divorce is the beginning of a whole new set of problems.

I've had my own mind battles. There are times in my marriage that the vow I pledged back in 1988 was the only thing holding me in place. I will go into this later on. But before we head into the foundation of marriage, which is commitment, let's look at a vision for marriage—a picture of what marriage is.

What Your Marriage Could Be

One of the greatest memories of my childhood is playing with my brothers underneath the old Hooker Oak Tree. Located in a park near my home in Chico, California, the oak tree was almost a hundred feet tall with a trunk 29 feet in circumference. The massive tree was a draw to many, especially children, who played under its canopy. I have vivid memories of swinging from the branches that curled downward almost to the ground, some with large cement markers propped up beneath to keep them from breaking. Experts at the time considered Hooker Oak to be the oldest valley oak in the country, approximately 1,000 years old.

When I was eleven, the Hooker Oak fell. As tree experts were called in to examine why this occurred, a shocking discovery was made. The Hooker Oak was not one tree, but actually two trees that had grown together over 300 years earlier.

Two trees that grew together over time, creating one large tree that brought life and beauty to those around and children frolicked beneath its shade. It was a picture of timeless strength.

Healthy marriages are like the Hooker Oak—two individuals growing together over time, creating one life that brings beauty and respite to those around. Children frolic beneath its strong protection. A great marriage is a picture of timeless strength.

As I've come into contact with police couples that have been married for long periods of time, there is strength there. They've been through a lot with the job and the kids and the grandkids. They have fought and loved and compromised and have had to work together on multiple levels through both difficulty and plenty. Their bond is unbreakable, and beautiful.

Your marriage can be like this. But it won't be easy. For our 27th anniversary, Brent stopped by to pick up flowers on the way home from work. As the florist worked on my bouquet, they talked about the benefits of a long time marriage. "You know that look old married people give each other?" he explained. "How they communicate with their eyes from across the room? It's not that their life was so happy all the time and easy. It's because they went through hell, and made it through together."

Well said, Babe!

Now, let's take a look at the foundation of a strong marriage—commitment.

Discussion Group Questions

1. Was your husband a police officer when you met? If yes, what were your impressions of his job? If no, what is the biggest change you saw in him when he became an officer?
2. Share one of your favorite on-duty stories your husband has told you.
3. What is the most difficult aspect of your husband's job that you struggle with?
4. What are some things you've done in your marriage which have helped with some of these struggles mentioned here?

CHAPTER 2

LOVERS, FIGHTERS, AND BACKUP: THE PARTNER'S ROLE

You can handle a lot more than you ever thought.
As long as he walks through your door at the
end of shift, nothing else really matters.
ERIKA, CALIFORNIA

You are the equivalent to an FTO[2]
for your cop's offline time.
TIMOTHY, WASHINGTON

t was Christmas Day when I realized our honeymoon was over. I hated our new apartment, I didn't know a soul, and I commuted to work an hour and a half each way through Los Angeles traffic. This place was very different from the small town of Chico where I grew up. On top of that, we had no money, a Charlie Brown Christmas tree we bought for eight bucks at a hardware store, and one gift from my grandparents. Brent was learning his new job in a difficult part of LA, and he worked swing shift on Christmas Eve. Me? Except for the manager's kids who came by to sing carols at my door (which I greatly appreciated), I spent it alone.

Earlier in December Brent graduated from the California Highway Patrol Academy, which was then and remains a residential training academy. We were given a week to move downstate and get settled before he reported for duty as a rookie officer in LA. Our six-month marriage was already experiencing a tough season.

---

2 Field Training Officer

We went from five months of weekend-only bliss to shift work and mandatory overtime. We left a small town of supportive family and friends to join a sea of unfamiliar faces and places. Our rent went up significantly, gas became a greater burden, and I had to work full time to make ends meet. We didn't know anyone except other new officers in the same boat. This was hard to handle all at once. But something else bothered me: Brent seemed to be changing, and not for the better.

Working on the streets of LA was affecting him. Brent had been a pre-med student and a church intern when I met him. He was tender and idealistic, but after he became a cop, he turned tough and painfully realistic. He saw some really disturbing things and couldn't share everything with me. His sweet demeanor was disappearing, and I didn't know what to do.

Suspecting I wasn't alone, I gingerly approached another newlywed wife whose husband graduated with Brent.

"Have you noticed a change in Bill lately?" I asked.

"What do you mean?" she replied.

"Well, it's hard to explain. Brent has kind of an edginess now that I haven't seen before. Some language, too. He seems frustrated and angry. Has Bill acted like this?"

She looked at me like I was purple and promptly shook her head. I walked away, sorry I ever mentioned it. *Well, that was helpful,* I thought to myself, embarrassed I'd made something out of nothing.

Three weeks later I was stunned to learn this same gal returned to her mother's home and filed for divorce. Obviously something was wrong, and she chose to shut up and get out. I wasn't giving in so easily. I decided at that moment that I would hold on tight to my man and find help.

But help was hard to find. It seemed everyone was tight-lipped about their relationships. And many of Brent's friends on the patrol were single. So I had to figure it out for myself.

I wondered what I'd gotten myself into. Suddenly I was married to someone different, and it wasn't what I had envisioned. But the one thing that carried me through this early season was the fact that I'd made a promise to Brent in front of God and everyone that I'd stay with him until "death do us part." I had to make it work.

Commit to Your Marriage

Every time I visit the grocery store, I'm reminded how easily promises are made and broken in relationships. While I am putting my food items on the conveyor belt, my eye is drawn to the magazines for the latest Hollywood gossip. This couple is history. That actor dumped his actress lover for another. Secret sexual trysts. Some of these people change partners as often as they change clothes.

I assume that not all of it is true. I understand that the drama is what sells. And I know that much of the world doesn't hold the same values as Hollywood. But because of the inundation of careless disregard for commitment that permeates our culture, we can't help but be influenced by it in our thinking. When a marriage experiences tough times, there are some who turn to other options way too soon.

Our wedding day was perfect. But two days before, we had the biggest fight we've had in our entire relationship. Brent and I spent several hours working through a fundamental issue that drew in several people in our wedding party. Looking back, I suppose we could've called it off. But we didn't. Because our minds were already geared that we were in it for keeps, we took the time to wrestle through the drama and get down to the core issue. After the tears dried, we were freed up to thoroughly enjoy our wedding and honeymoon. Even though we were very young, we understood "for better or worse."

Travis and Krista had been married for nine up-and-down years when Travis found someone whom he felt understood him more than Krista. Through small choices to open his soul to this woman, he chose to leave the commitment he'd made all those years earlier, moved out, and started what he thought would be a better life. It didn't turn out that way. Krista didn't let go. She fought for him, bringing in reinforcements. Though the hurt was deep, she decided that their marriage had been rough, but they could make it better with some changes. After a time, Travis came to his senses and moved back home. They had deep conversations for the first time. They pinpointed issues and vowed to work through them, which is exactly what they did. They recommitted themselves to their marriage and to each other, seeking the help of others to help them resolve those issues. They are now stronger than ever, helping others who find themselves in the same boat.

True and unwavering commitment requires a purposeful steeling of the mind. It's an attitude that doesn't consider divorce an option. And it is the glue that will hold a couple together through the messiest of times.

The Escape Clause

It doesn't matter how awesome your officer is; there will be a time when your mind will be tempted to entertain other options. Boredom, loneliness, a grass-is-greener moment, another handsome uniform—there are lots of temptations that come along that threaten your marital commitment. If your mind isn't engaged for the long haul, it could get you into trouble.

When I married Brent, I gave my whole heart to him. Or so I thought. A year or two into our marriage, I realized that there was a little spot inside me that I reserved for the "what if". What if he is killed on duty? What if he leaves me for someone else? These were fears that I held in the back of my mind. For a time, I developed a place to retreat to in my mind, just in case these fears came to life. I call this protective inner wall the escape clause. And when things got a little tough, I'd retreat behind that wall and let my mind wander. I'd put together a plan. Where I'd go, how I'd react, and, sometimes, whom I'd consider dating if Brent were gone. Eventually I challenged myself to stay away from the escape clause; it made my commitment waver. And when things got more difficult, I didn't need the temptation to run.

The escape clause has to be taken in context. I am referring to secret thoughts of a woman that are meant to protect but actually hinder her from commitment and complete intimacy. These thoughts are based on a fear of being hurt. By no means am I referring to a relationship in which the husband is abusing his wife emotionally, physically, or sexually. In these situations, there are cases in which separation can actually save a marriage.

Buckle Up

Are you all in? Or will you balk when hard times put you to the test? Are you willing to take courageous, proactive steps to nurture that commitment? I will talk more about these steps in Chapter 12, but for now fasten your seatbelt!

Your seatbelt of commitment, that is. A seatbelt is protection we depend on every time we get in the car. It may seem a bit confining or claustrophobic to some, but it's necessary. Our husbands can attest to accidents they've seen that, had the victims worn seatbelts, they would've been a lot better off. In many cases it is the difference between life and death. When trouble comes, it is the one thing that holds us in place when all else is sliding every which way. In like manner, commitment does the very same thing.

But you have to choose to put it on ahead of time. Trying to do so at the moment of impact is impossible. It's too late.

Commit to the Job

Before your husband was allowed to pin his badge on his uniform, he had to swear an oath to protect and to serve the people of his jurisdiction. Here are a couple examples:

> I will support and defend the Constitution of the United States against all enemies, foreign and domestic; that I will bear true faith and allegiance to the same; that I take this obligation freely, without any mental reservation or purpose of evasion; and that I will well and faithfully discharge the duties of the office on which I am about to enter. So help me God.
> FBI[1]

> To serve the United States of America and the State of California honestly, and conscientiously; and fulfill my oath as a soldier of the law; To uphold and maintain the honor and integrity of the California Highway Patrol; Be loyal to my fellow officers; respect and obey my seniors in rank; and enforce the law without fear, favor, or discrimination; Assist those in peril or distress, and, if necessary, lay down my life rather than swerve from the path of duty; My personal conduct shall at all times be above reproach and I will never knowingly commit any act that will in any way

bring discredit upon the California Highway Patrol or any member thereof; To all of this I do solemnly pledge my sacred honor as an Officer of the California Highway Patrol.
CHP[2]

The oath your husband swore as a peace officer affects you whether you like it or not. At times this oath will take precedence over things that are very important to you—birthday parties, family dinners, and holidays, to name a few. And it's easy to resent your husband's job when a couple of missed events stack up. This oath can be a foe, or, with the right mindset, it can be a friend. At the very least, we can make peace with it.

It's your choice. When he's running "all roads, all codes" with his hair on fire, will you commit yourself to accept not only the benefits of his job but also the consequences? I may be sounding a bit like Officer Negative (see Introduction), but he was right; marriage *is* hard. Being a cop's spouse is even harder. But what does commitment look like?

To commit to his job means choosing a good attitude when he's at the jail late and you have to put the kids to bed by yourself. It means talking out your frustrations with him at an appropriate time instead of as he's heading out the door for his shift. It is knowing full well that it may have to be this way until he catches that thief or arrests that killer. It means slipping into survival mode for a time to make things work. It may mean growing up a bit, having your own needs take a back seat to the pressing issues of his job for a time. But then, at the appropriate occasion, voice your concerns courageously instead of stuffing them inside to fester. Committing to his job means knowing that seasons come and go, persevering, and looking forward. This is tough to do and will take some practice, so let me give you more perspective on this idea.

Partners at Home

Shortly after I started writing this book, word spread about what I was doing. I got a phone call one morning from a sergeant in our employee assistance unit with her full support. She told me that the timing was right for my book, as "the face of law enforcement is changing. We are discovering more and more the importance of emotional care for our officers, and we're doing something about it. The families are a big component of that." Since then, the past seven years have brought more and more awareness and acceptance of emotional care for officers. As we look at challenges in law enforcement such as divorce, alcoholism, PTSD, and suicide, we're finding answers. And true to the sergeant's word, the family is definitely a big part of the solution.

My husband and I knew this instinctively early on in our marriage. He told me from the beginning that he couldn't do this without me. I believed it then and even more so now. Your spouse can go through the academy, train, and save lives, but there is another side of him that really needs you. Your respect can bolster his confidence. Your support can give him that extra emotional stability that he will need as his job wears him down. Your love can break down the walls he'll be tempted to build around himself when what he sees hurts his sense of how the world should be. It may seem a little overstated to some, but when I say you are a not-so-silent partner behind the badge, our everyday reality shows it to be true.

Understanding your role in the big picture can help you deal with the negative pieces of his job and convince you to commit to the cause. There is something to be said about the satisfaction in being a part of something bigger than yourself.

Commit to the Adventure

Solemn commitments are there for the long haul, put in place for the protection of you, your husband, and your marriage. But there are many seasons of pure enjoyment and fulfillment! There are many positive things about being the wife of a police officer. I chose a long time ago to look at our life together as an adventure. I chose a life of ups and downs, twists and turns, highs, lows, and everything in between. And most of the time, I love it!

Let me share a few of our memories over the years:

I remember turning beat red when a large group of cadets sang "Happy Birthday" to me on the steps of our state capitol. That was definitely cool.

We missed a wedding in Northern California and drove all night to SoCal when Brent decided to return to help with the LA riots even though we were on vacation. Somehow I felt his call of duty and chose to answer it with my full support. There's a satisfaction I have when I recount it now, like I did the right thing for the greater good. Maybe you understand?

When it was time to move, I accepted it, looking forward to a new adventure, and kept in touch with those we left behind. Now I have friends in several parts of the state, and I've never regretted it.

I cried when a twenty-year-old killed her two best friends when she decided to drive drunk.

I laugh as I remember how a poker game in the backyard became a little more eventful when a mole chose to run through a crowd of cigar-smoking cops. Bad move for the rodent. There was one less pest in the world to dig up our lawn!

When my two-year-old son burned his hands after falling into a camp-fire, Brent's coworkers put together a basket of goodies for him to pass the time with while he healed. The support of other officers and office personnel has been huge when hard times hit.

When a call came in of a nearby pursuit while having a deep con-versation at home with out-of-state friends, I quickly helped Brent climb into his uniform and watched him screech away (he was the on-call supervisor). Our friends and I later listened with wild anticipation as he recounted how the pursuit ended in a field of flames with the suspect in custody. Hoorah!

I clapped as tears filled my eyes when I witnessed an incredible victory over tragedy. Months after one of our officers became a paraplegic when he was hit on duty, he hand-pedaled his specialized bike as he joined my husband and his cadets on a run to the state capitol.

I enjoyed being in the know when my husband got to be involved in a high-profile case. He was the first officer on the scene where two of the three victims were recovered in the highly publicized Yosemite murders.

I fervently prayed three years for Brent through a difficult season of his career, and I was the first one he came to when he started to see some resolution.

It has been an honor and a pleasure to walk with police families through crises these past years. As we've grown in our marriage, we've been able to listen and share insight to younger couples. This truly has been the deepest satisfaction.

These are just a few of our memories. Your list has no doubt started and grows by the year. From time to time, it feels good to recount the ups and downs like I've done here. It bolsters confidence, knowing that we survived the downs intact, coming away with a little more strength, a little more wisdom. The ups invite an attitude of thankfulness, enjoying the good times once again.

It's a wild and crazy adventure, a very full life. Know that more great things will be added in the years to come if you commit to the adventure. You'll be glad you did.

The Life Partner's Role

As our officer's closest relationship, we have an incredible opportunity as spouses, and responsibility. You and I know our officers intimately. We know how they think, and why they act the way they do. As life partners of an officer, we are our spouse's backup. While we don't grab a gun and drive CODE 3 to rescue them in their dire need, there are four specific ways I've seen that we can backup our officers: relationally, practically, mentally, and emotionally.

The first is that we are our officer's **compass**. A compass indicates where we are in reference to true north. You know your spouse in "normal state." As they move off course in some way because of the job or otherwise, we are the first to know it and can point it out.

Second, we are our officer's **safe place**. Eight to twelve plus hours a day, our officers serve, with each call or "routine stop" offering unknown danger. They are given weapons and body armor for a reason. They've been trained with safety in mind and must remain vigilant the entire shift. Providing a home and a demeanor that welcomes them in makes all the difference. They need a safe place to rest, recharge, and relate to those who love and support them. We want to be that place that our officers want to come home to.

Third, we have an important **voice**. Because we are that compass, we have to find our voice and speak words that need to be heard—reassurance, exhortation, encouragement, and sometimes, words that are harder to hear. I had to find my voice over the years because of how I was raised. Others may not have any trouble letting their voice be heard. If this describes you, use your voice wisely, making sure that nagging, complaining, and whining give way to rational thoughts and words. And with all, being eager to listen and slow to speak from anger.

The final way we can provide backup to our spouse is **balance**. Officers tend to eat and sleep the job. Constant contact with who police have to deal with day in and day out can jade them. Everyone's a dirtbag. Everyone is a liar. Boy Scout leaders are pedophiles. You get it...but it's not the whole population. You and I have a different outlook; we generally deal with decent and good people. Our perspectives matter, and have a way to balance the negativity from the job.

Your Value

I once heard Melissa Littles (The Police Wife Life) speak about her journey to pass legislation to protect police officers. She saw some victories, but then the lack of implementation afterward was very frustrating. What she took away from that experience is that the most important support for police officers was not legislation, or leadership within the department, or even the public—it was within their very own homes! You and I have a vital role as support for the thin blue line. Each of us is uniquely suited to be a valuable force of strength with our families, and our communities.

With this thought in mind I wrote a poem about police wives. I heard the voices of other cop wives and it seemed like many of them were fighting for their marriages, for their officer's wellbeing, and for their kids. Some days I feel the same.

Warriors at Home
We are the warriors behind those who go to war.

While our officers battle on the streets, we battle from within our homes. We are the strong back up forces that support, equip, and empower our police officers out on the street.

We support.
We know what they go through; we know the cost. We let them lean on us for what they need so they can do what they do out there, coming home at the end of the shift.

We defend.
We battle the questions. There are those who are against our officers, who hate their authority to take away their ability to wreak havoc on our communities and families. It's hard to hear the criticism, even from those we are close to. But we stand up for our officers anyway, sometimes with silent strength.

We fear.
There are many unknowns that we face. Will he come home? Will he be faithful? Will he be safe? We have no guarantees. We endure close calls, hospitals, the what ifs.

We do without.
We are lonely, we are underestimated, we are thought of as weak. But it takes an amazing person to do without and creatively thrive anyway.

We go alone.
We go to birthday parties, school plays, and church services. We get dressed and put on makeup and smile, knowing that our officer can't be there. We would prefer to go with our officer—but instead we just go.

We face hard moments alone.
We take our kids to the doctor, and take the phone call of bad news. We walk on eggshells when our officer is bothered by something and wait patiently for him to spill the reason. We face hard moments knowing that our officer will be there, eventually.

We make do.
We explain to our little ones why their daddies or mommies aren't there. We've already wrestled with this in our minds and hearts. It's not how

we'd like it to be. But it is reality, and the first thing a cop spouse must do is to accept things as they are.

We cry.

Tears are not a sign of weakness; they are a sign of strength. We acknowledge that sometimes life sucks, and we are not made of stone. But we are strong—strong enough to let ourselves be soft when we need to be.

We mourn.

We put on black and we tuck a handkerchief in our pockets and we stand with our officers and mourn those who made the ultimate sacrifice. We hurt with our husbands, and feel their pain, and let the tears flow when they're not around. We feel the pain, too.

We cope.

When things go sideways and catastrophes happen, we learn to roll with it. We cope. We make things happen. We thrive when others only survive. And we do what we must.

We stand.

We know who our officers are and who they are not, yet we stand with them through the darkest of hours and the brightest of victories.

We work hard.

We clean and cook and plan and flex and work because we believe that what we do matters to our family. We work hard to make a safe place for our officer to come home to, day in, day out, year in, year out.

We trust.

We believe in the training and abilities that our officers have. We trust them to be safe, and to be vigilant. We trust their partners to watch their back, and their leaders to do the same. We choose to trust in the face of fear.

We are loyal.
We care about our officers, and we are in their camp. We love them fiercely and defend them to those who would dare speak or act against them.

We are proud.
We love the uniform and all it represents. We know the need, we see the sacrifice, and know what our officer did to earn his uniform, his badge, his gun, and pride in who he is.

We persevere.
At times it is tiresome. There are times when we are lonely, and we are exhausted, and we are done, and yet we wake up every morning and do it again. And again. And again.

We fight.
But we fight anyway. We fight for our marriages. We fight for our families. We fight for our rights. We fight our own emotions and we fight with our officers. There is no place for us on the sidelines.

We love fiercely.
This is our motivation and our perseverance.

We are warriors.

We are strong.

Discussion Group Questions

1. What is it that you like about your husband's job?
2. What are some memorable moments from his career that come to mind?

3. How do you feel about being a not-so-silent partner behind the badge?

4. Do you struggle with the escape clause? Elaborate.

5. Which of the three commitments do you need help in? What is one way you can improve?

CHAPTER 3

CREATING YOUR OWN NORMAL

*I think you have to kinda let go of the life that you
thought you were gonna have when you marry an
officer. I really do. I think you have to realize that you
are in a new life now. And it's gonna throw you curves.
It's different than any other job there is out there.*
JENNY, CALIFORNIA

*Have a sense of humor, a filter, backbone, funny
bone, and cell phone. Learn when to just listen,
when to speak, and when to lie beside him and
just be. If they are brave enough to suit up,
we have to be brave enough to let them.*
PAULA, TEXAS

*Be a big girl...it takes a special woman to be in a
relationship with an LEO. Be independent...learn to go
with the flow...the job often comes first, but be strong
enough to know that he loves you. Do not whine and
complain—he needs a strong woman in his corner!*
LAINE, CALIFORNIA

There is no normal. Not really. Gone are the days where we compare
ourselves to the Cleavers or the Joneses. We are a creative people
collectively. If you took a survey of the households on your street, you
might find that someone comes or goes all twenty-four hours of the day.

Living in the city, I am always amazed how many people are out and about at four in the morning.

We create our own normal. My normal may be vastly different from your normal. The challenge comes when we try to make plans with others or even those within our own household. With teenagers and young adults in and out of our home, dinners around the table with everyone present are rare. Sports and work schedules prohibit many nights together. When they were smaller, the kids and I had dinner together every night, and normal was either Brent was there, or we kept a plate heated for later. In both situations everyone appreciates when we do have everyone present, and it's usually a really fun night.

Before Brent and I had children, he worked swings (1400 to 2300, military time), and I worked at an office (0800 to 1700). We each were alone for several hours—he in the morning, I in the evening. We chose to look at it positively; we got to see each other at least four days a week. And we took advantage of those moments together and apart. We created our own normal.

DeAnn and Shawn both work and have two busy children. Their lives are very full with four schedules to juggle. It was quickly becoming unmanageable, so DeAnn bought a whiteboard to put on the wall in the kitchen. Everyone's schedule was placed on the calendar. It was Shawn's responsibility to get his work schedule on the whiteboard in a timely manner. From then on, she was able to be organized and keep the details of the family straight.

I keep two calendars. A large desktop calendar worked the best for me when the kids were younger; they wrote in their events and checked on dates themselves. Brent uses Google for his schedule. After several conflicts in communication, Brent asked if I could sync our computers/phones by inputting events on a joined Gmail calendar. It works perfectly as long as I input things in a timely manner! We add in the kids' information when they are home.

Balancing Home Life and Career(s)

Jenny and Tim had been married double-digit years when they had their first child. Before this time she was a dispatcher and he an officer. They worked out their shifts together, and it was relatively easy, considering it was just the two of them. But when their daughter came, things changed. Jenny quit her job to stay home. Tim was still working long hours, and there were other demands that had to be taken care of as well.

In response they set up an agreement. They decided that when he had his days off, he was to give them one full day. The other days were up for grabs, but one day was to be spent with his girls. This worked as they scheduled several days a month to be together. It was intentional, quality time.

Kathy and Jerry did something similar. Jerry would come home from long hours on the job and retreat to the computer. He checked his email, browsed Facebook, and then played games for hours. But it was creating resentment in Kathy. He'd already been gone for many hours; why would he want to spend more time without her and their son? She came to understand that he, in fact, craved that down time; he needed to think through the demands he felt during his shift. But this understanding didn't entirely solve their problem. What did work was scheduling time to sit together and talk without other distractions. Sometimes they'd talk about their days, other times they got into deep issues, and other times they planned special trips. And occasionally these nice little talks led to intimacy in the bedroom.

Seasons: Recreating Normal

As the years progress, seasons come and go. Seasons of long hours. Seasons of illness. Seasons with children. Seasons with inadequate leadership within the department. Some of these seasons are amazing and some are excruciating. But they come and they go. When we live day to day, it's very easy to forget this.

I took a walk with a physical trainer several years ago. Kate was bemoaning the fact that she was to have surgery on her knee within the week. She was weary of her injury. She was worried about gaining weight and possibly losing her job. She was sure that life would crumble around her and never be the same.

I suggested that she was in a winter season. I explained that there are seasons of life that seem bleak. Colorless. Like there's no hope. She perked up when I told her that winter seasons eventually move into spring seasons. Seasons that show promise of beauty and color. There's newness everywhere, and we get excited in our anticipation. Spring seasons move into summer seasons, and so on. Kate told me she'd never heard that before but seemed hopeful. Two months later she led our water aerobics class in a full-hour workout. Spring had come.

It's all about attitude.

If you understand and accept who you are, seeing the value you add to your marriage and family, your attitude will reflect that. Obstacles? Yes. Challenges? Absolutely. But when you understand difficulty is a part of this life, and meet them with a positive but realistic attitude, you're on the right path.

But what if your attitude sucks? I've been there—dealing with disappointment again and again gets me down sometimes. Thoughts are powerful. They have influence over our emotions, our demeanor, and our relationships. Add in hormones (my son called them "horrormones" when he was nine), and suddenly the clouds roll in, the sky grows dark, and we are under a blanket of discouragement. It's at these times that we have to be patient, untangling our thoughts.

Every Thanksgiving weekend we open the boxes of ornaments for our Christmas tree. Every year it's the same thing—tangled lights that I sloppily threw in the January before. *Oh, I'll deal with this later*, I think. They're a mess! The first thing I have to do is untangle them, laying them out straight and replacing bulbs so I can use them again.

Like the light strands, we have to first straighten out our thoughts— what are they and where do they come from? Why am I feeling this way? Once my thoughts are straight, some parts may need clarity—and that may require more communication or more information. Once those thoughts are clear, it's time to either find ways to overcome those obstacles, or make peace with them.

If your husband is low man on the totem pole and has to work the undesirable shifts, or is working really long hours because of a case he's on, it will end at some point. Some seasons are longer than others, but they do change. Your attitude makes the difference. Understand that you have to create a new normal for each season. Adjust expectations. Hold onto hope. Hunker down and persevere during the winter, knowing that spring is on its way.

Sometimes You Just Have To Be Brave

The laughter was deafening. Emily found herself laughing along; although because she didn't really know these people, she felt a touch uncomfortable. Clara had just opened her white-elephant gift: a set of five condoms. It was definitely appropriate for the crowd. They were all recently married, and everyone's husband or wife was present. That is, everyone's spouse but Emily's. Emily's husband was on duty.

It was her turn. She looked over the gifts that were beautifully wrapped underneath the tree. She chose a gorgeous red box tied with a silver bow. As she started to poke at the ribbon, she thought she heard a guy whisper, "Oh, no." Too late!

At first when Emily opened the box, she had no idea what it was. She lifted it out, and, of course, everyone howled. "What *is* this?" she asked.

Her face flushed crimson as she heard someone shout, "Edible underwear!"

Sometimes you just have to be brave. When events come up, and your husband is working, go. You never know what that event may hold! There will be times when your loneliness will increase because you really wish he were there. But, more often than not, you'll make a memory. Or laugh trying. Sometimes you'll even gain a new friend.

When Brent was a cadet in the academy, I drove home after visiting him in Sacramento. It was very dark, and I was on a stretch of rural highway in the middle of nowhere. Suddenly my car sputtered, coughed, jerked a few times, and I found myself rolling, powerless, to the side of the road. Annoyed, I got out of the car, went around to the front, and froze. I saw small flames flickering underneath. In a panic I lost all sense of safety and waved my arms at a few cars that came by. Finally a young man stopped, put out the fire with some water he had in his car, and assured me everything was okay. There was a spooky-looking house several yards away, and about that time, a flashlight approached. "Do ya need to use a phone?" the creepy resident asked. I flashed a look of fear to the young man, and he accompanied me into the house while I called a tow truck and family. An hour later I was on my way home.

This was the first time I had to solve a problem like this all by myself. It was scary! Brent was unavailable, my dad was out of town, and I had to grow up and deal. It was good for me. Since that night I can't tell you how many times I've had to take care of problems on my own: hospital visits, car repairs, issues with teachers, landlords, and tenants, you name it. Brent helps me when he can, but, for the most part, I've learned I can hold down the fort quite well.

It would be easy to resent situations like these. It would be easy to resent him for not being there. But a sense of survival or duty can take over if you allow it. In fact, you can even choose to gain a sense of accomplishment from learning new skills. This is the kind of strength we can use to build our new normal.

A word of caution here: Law enforcement draws certain kinds of people, and many have a deeply set rescuer mentality. Our guys want to be needed and valued as an important part of the family. We must keep this in mind, making sure that we don't become so independent that we cease to need them, as tempting as that can be sometimes. I'm talking about balance here, and there is no formula. We have to figure this out with our spouses. Interdependence is the goal, but when our cops aren't able to do something, we have to pick up the slack.

Make It Work!

Christmas doesn't have to be celebrated Christmas morning. The Fourth of July picnic can be on the third, and you'll enjoy it more with less people around! Vacations don't have to be in the summer months. And days off don't have to be on Saturday and Sunday.

Vacations, holidays, and schedules are yours to tweak to make it work. Each season of your life will have additional considerations. But if you're willing to think outside the box, you'll be surprised how well events turn out.

Brent always liked to work Christmas Eve. It was generally quiet, so he'd have the guys who didn't have families nearby come to the house even if we had other guests. He asked me to "work my magic" in the kitchen and spoil them with flavor. I loved every minute of it. We have very fond memories of candles from the table casting a warm glow on their badges. And there was always laughter with a cop at the table.

A Word to the New

If you are brand new to this police career and all it entails, you may feel a bit overwhelmed. But take heart—it's a transition. There will be things that change. There will be things you don't like. There will be days you'll have to put on your big-girl pants! But you're not alone. There are others just like you who've been there before. We've done that and got the T-shirt, and most important, we've lived long enough to tell the story! Some of those stories once drew tears, but now they draw laughter and sometimes even pride. And the amount of resources available for your family now is amazing—and growing!

Your officer went through a period of time to learn how to be a police officer. He went through academy training, break-in training, and then was on probation as he learned to implement on the streets what he'd learned from the classroom. The more experience he gets, the better cop he'll be. The same goes for you. You can do your research on what it's like to be a LEOW (your new acronym)[3]. You can talk to those who've been there. But the day will come when you'll have on-the-job training. Soon you'll be fully immersed, and it'll be second nature.

As you begin life with your officer (whether he's new, or you are), try to hold on to four things:

1. Flexibility—Bend, don't break. Learn to hold onto expectations loosely.
2. Attitude—It's yours to control. A positive one is easier to carry.
3. Communication—It's a two-way street. Keep traffic moving!
4. Tenacity—Don't give up. Don't give up. Don't. Give. Up.

---

3 Law Enforcement Officer's Wife

Expectations For All

If you expect that your life is supposed to look like your dad's office job, you will be disappointed. If you expect your husband to make every single event you plan and on time, you will be disappointed. If you don't try to be creative in making memories that include your officer, you will be disappointed. If you refuse to solve some of the problems that arise when he's on duty, you'll be frustrated.

The attitude of strength here is flexibility. Creating your own normal and recreating normal are an integral part of a long-lasting law-enforcement marriage. Choosing to be flexible and optimistic in the face of unmet expectations is tough at times, but necessary. Managing those expectations with flexibility and optimism ahead of time is even better. Communicating those expectations is another matter altogether.

Discussion Group Questions

1. What does normal look like in your family right now?
2. Name one idea that you came up with to incorporate your husband's job with your family time.
3. What was one expectation you came into your marriage with that didn't pan out?
4. Share about a winter experience and what spring looked like.

CHAPTER 4

GAME FACE: UNDERSTANDING YOUR OFFICER

*I've always been an independent person. It is at times extremely difficult to respect my husband's wishes concerning what he believes to be things that are important to my safety. Hypervigilance is a part of who he is, and it isn't going away...my husband bears an incredible amount of responsibility on his shoulders and is answerable to God for it. It is my duty and responsibility as his wife to help him shoulder that burden as best I can, and that means respecting his wishes...I am not a victim and I am not controlled by him. My choice to respect him is **my choice**, and it has served our relationship very well.*

HAYLEY, TENNESSEE

Don't get upset about everything that pertains to the job. Don't say, "I hate your job." The job is tough. They need your support...they will see/hear/do things that place a heavy burden on them.

SERENA, TEXAS

Michelle sat on the bed, watching Greg dress. She chattered away, recounting a conversation from dinner with girlfriends the night before. Irritated, Greg looked at her with that cop-look in his eye and scolded, "Not the time." He shoved his gun in the holster and walked out.

How many times have we witnessed a form of this scenario? They're getting ready for work, and we're enjoying their last few minutes at home. But somehow we innocently manage to irritate them, and then there is conflict right before they leave! It took years for me to understand that when my husband puts on his uniform and weaponry, he has to put on his mind armor as well. That changes his demeanor. Once he's dressed, he's on duty—including his mind. Things of home fade to background.

We want them to do this. Not because we enjoy the conflict, or want to feel defensive. But because we want them to come home unharmed!

What they do requires body and mind, even a little of the soul. It's a war mentality to steel the mind to deal with whatever will come their way that shift. Even harmless chitchat can be irritating as they put on the game face. They must be on their game mentally—more now than ever.

Understanding the Cop Mentality

To be a cop is to be many different occupations all at once. He has to be an athlete, a soldier, a scientist, a researcher, a paramedic, a NASCAR driver, a gun expert and marksman, a counselor, a chemist, a diplomat, a wrestler, a runner, a mechanic, a writer, and a lawyer. He must have a mother's intuition, the nose of a bloodhound, the patience of a farmer, the compassion of Mother Teresa, and the tenacity of a two-year-old. He must make peace out of chaos, comfort the anguished, discern criminal behavior from stupidity, and make split second decisions that may have life-altering consequences. He's expected to be polite when verbally abused, keep people safe in dangerous situations, respect those who disrespect him, and understand the intentions of those who are misbehaving. He must constantly confront evil, and remain unsullied. He must be quick to respond, though sometimes the calls stack up. He must be able to speak police shorthand on radios that may be difficult to hear, especially when in heavy or fast-moving traffic. He is constantly second guessed on his actions, criticized for his demeanor, mocked for his diet and feared for his authority. He's a threat, a target, a punisher, yet is a rescuer, a protector, and in some cases, a savior.

Given these considerations, society's expectations on our law enforcement are just short of impossible. Since Ferguson, the pressure has gotten ridiculous. But day to day they report for duty, not knowing what the shift will offer. They put on their badges and try to do the best they can to fulfill the expectations of those they serve.

With these pressures in mind, it's our privilege to be not-so-silent partners behind the badge. Our influence backs them up where they tank up, gear up, and man up to be who they need to be and to do what they're expected to do.

Understanding His Motivation

"War is seductive. There's something inside me that lures me to the mission. I look at what's goin' down and know that I have to do what it takes to rescue these men... It's almost like I have this need, deep inside of me..." The soldier's eyes were moist and serious like he was reliving his combat experience again. I could see the pain on his face as images flashed through his mind's eye.

"And then, as I heard the bullets whiz by my head, I came to my senses. What am I doing? I have kids... I have a job at home... why am I taking these risks?"

It was a crowded room, but I didn't notice anything else. It was the closest thing I'd heard yet that describes the warrior mentality. Although I couldn't step into his shoes, it resonated within me. Duty. Compassion. Laying down one life for another. Courage that comes from deep within. I'd seen glimpses of this before in my husband and his co-workers. This is the mind of a man in uniform.

Some are born with it. Some learn it really young when they're watching Daddy put on his badge. Some are enticed by the honor and respect that goes with the shield and gun. No matter where they got it, it's there. It's a powerful, inner force that drives them on.

Sheep, Wolves and Sheepdogs

Perhaps the best description of the differences between civilians, criminals, and officers is by Lt. Col. Dave Grossman. He describes civilians as sheep, criminals as wolves, and law enforcement/military as sheepdogs. I explain this in an excerpt of a blog post I wrote in September 2012 called, "Sorry, No Lamb Chops Today!":

Why do some people hate cops so much?

Why does a man see a young officer on the side of the road tending to a dead deer, pull over, and come out shooting? Where does that rage come from?

A few days prior, a fellow LEO wife had her husband's uniform hanging in her car, and decided to stop at 7-11 on her way home from the dry cleaners. Four scumbags nearby commented rather loudly, "That guy should've taken out more cops before he got gunned down in cold blood." Where does that come from? It sends shivers down my spine. (And it's a reminder to all of us LEOWs to put the dry cleaning in the trunk).

I've been thinking about this quite a bit. Asking God about it.

I drove myself to [CHP Officer Kenyon Youngstrom's] funeral yesterday. My car didn't look like the others that were parked on every flat surface a half-mile radius around the church. And I watched cops arrive from every direction. They were intimidating. Chiseled faces, helmets and caps, sunglasses, shiny badges, lights flickering, weapons around their waists. Because I'm sorta into this kinda thing, I got this warm feeling inside. Wow! But what about others who got caught in the traffic jam? Did the same view that gives me warm fuzzies give them a sense of dread? I'd be willing to bet yes.

There are three different kinds of people in this world. There are sheep, wolves, and sheepdogs.

The sheep are the biggest group—they live quiet lives meal to meal, don't care about much that doesn't affect their world, and just want to be safe and happy.

The wolves want to prey on the sheep. Devour them. Satiate their thirst for blood and death. Most predators don't care if it gets messy.

And then there are the sheepdogs that make up only 2% of the population. They're a little confusing. They look like predators on the outside (cute, yes, but look at their sharp teeth), but their motivation—their job—is to keep the sheep safe. They stand in the way of danger and say to the wolves that they will not feast on the sheep. They stand in the way of danger, and say to the wolves, YOU WILL NOT EAT. And how do you think those wolves feel about that? Probably strong enough to randomly pull over on the side of the road and kill him.

Do you think the sheep are happy the sheepdogs are around? You'd think so. And some are. But sometimes those sheepdogs get a little bossy. Sometimes the sheepdogs have to get after the sheep because they're doing something stupid that could jeopardize their safety. And because of that, sheep aren't always grateful. Instead, they're irritated.

Sometimes sheepdogs die protecting the sheep. Not gladly, but willingly. And those of us who commit to our sheepdogs understand the risks. But we love them anyway.

Because they're people. Humans who tear up when it's safe to do so. They love, and laugh, and feel deeply and play, but they are still sheepdogs at the core of their being. And when they put on the uniform, they tell wolves, NO LAMBCHOPS TODAY.

There are some that reason that if there were no sheepdogs, there would be no wolves. If we lay our weapons down, if we just learn to understand, be nice, try not to offend, then the wolves will go away. But if our cops cease to exist, it doesn't mean the wolves will go prancing into the sunset with nothing to do.

It means they will devour the sheep.[4]

Only two percent of the general population can do what our husbands do. They are willing to complete what's necessary in each situation. They may even lay down their lives to stop a criminal from producing chaos and death, and that willingness commands respect. Do you respect your husband for who he is? For what he values?

---

4 http://www.how2loveyourcop.com/sorry-no-lamb-chops-today/

My friend Deidra has had a difficult time with this in her twenty-year marriage. He may be a hero out on the road, but it wasn't always the case at home. She and I had a conversation and this is what she said:

In their line of work, they get respect. When people see a cop, they definitely clean up their act a little. Then he comes home, and I don't give him that respect. Why don't I give him that respect? Because some of the things he says are not respectful! When you're acting like a jerk, why should I respect you?

One of my biggest failures has been that I haven't valued him. I haven't valued his accomplishments, the fact that he is putting his life on the line for other people, that he's a great provider, a great husband, and a great father. When I don't respect him, he feels really bad about himself. And that affects a lot of things, like our relationship. He feels like a failure because he thinks I don't believe in him. They get this level of respect on the road, and then when they get home, we don't give it. I think it's degrading. I wish I could go back and do it over again… to be more proud of him. I am proud of him.

Diedra and her cop have been married a long time and have a good marriage. But she is realizing now that the way she treats him affects him as a man and as a police officer. Respect is to a man what love is to a woman. It's their greatest need. We as wives can remember that there is always something to value within our husbands even when they're not faring well in other areas. It helps to remember him as a whole rather than honing in on his weaknesses.

Understanding His Moods

In his book *Emotional Survival for Law Enforcement Officers*, Dr. Kevin Gilmartin describes the highs and lows of what he calls the hypervigilance rollercoaster. To be vigilant is to stay watchful and alert to danger or trouble. But because our officers never know what will come at them on any given call, they maintain a state of hypervigilance throughout their shift. They are programmed for survival to overcome whatever they deal with while on duty, and that requires much more than just a pep talk to themselves as they go out the door.

Their bodies and minds sustain this level of hypervigilance throughout the shift. But what goes up must come down, even physiologically. After his shift is over, he retreats home to you and your family, but his mind and body are exhausted from maintaining a high level of watchful intensity. Rather than returning to a normal level, his mind and body go to a place below normal to recuperate. The symptoms are depression-like, heading for the nearest chair in front of the nearest screen. The next day it's repeated. And the next. Eventually, this wears him (and you!) down. The kids wonder why daddy is acting this way. Everyone walks on eggshells, and the elephant in the room has control of the remote. A precious wife once asked me with tears in her eyes, "What do I do? I feel like I'm losing him!" I told her to stand in front of the TV!

Thing is, this hypervigilance rollercoaster isn't healthy for the family, and it isn't good for your officer's mental, emotional, and physical health. Without intervention, this constant up and down behavior will cause all kinds of health problems. It also isolates your officer from those closest to him—and isolation is the enemy.

If you have an understanding of what is going on inside his body and mind, the good news is you are a big component of helping him through it. Dr. Gilmartin says,

> ...[T]he rollercoaster sets up officers to think, act, and live like victims, to not invest their energy, emotions, and sense of self in the phase of the rollercoaster that they do in fact control, the bottom or off-duty phase. It's a clear catch-22: Officers must maintain hypervigilance to perform and survive on the streets and practice good officer safety, yet it is this same hypervigilance that can cause officers to relinquish control of their personal lives. They cannot lower the upper phase of the rollercoaster. They must maintain the elevated physical state of heightened awareness of potential risk while functioning as officers. Without training and awareness of the rollercoaster, officers return home and experience the pendulum effect... *Ironically, it is the non-police support systems that, when they remain intact, determine if the officers*

remain good cops for the duration of the entire police career...
(Emphasis mine.)[5]

You are the first and foremost non-police support system. Understanding this process gives you a chance to deal with it. You can help him maintain balance by creating balance. Things like dinner at the table, exercise, vacations, hobbies, and activities will pull him out of that below normal level his body wants to retreat to. Take time to rejuvenate as a couple and as a family during his off-duty time, keeping this phenomenon in mind.

Before and After Shifts

Many times this hypervigilance rollercoaster will begin just before he leaves for work. He's putting on his game face. For Brent and I, the time before his shift wasn't pretty for years. Sometimes I'd be upset half the shift after he'd leave. He was intensely focused. There were a few hurt feelings here and there. I finally learned he needed his space to gear up for the day. It wasn't directed at me. He was inwardly focused to be on his game.

I also needed to be careful about the demands I placed on him right before work. A half hour before he was to leave was not a good time to talk about bills or problems with the kids or scheduling conflicts. I learned to make a list for later. A little patience and everyone benefits.

For many officers, coming home is a lot of the same. In addition to that coming down from hypervigilance, a bad accident, a supervisor's comment, or an incident involving children will sometimes bother your officer, and he needs a little space to think it through before reengaging at home. When something like this arises, are we aware and sensitive to his demeanor? Random questions or requests may conflict with his ability to process those particularly hard days. You never know what he's dealt with that day. How do we handle their responses like strong, mature people?

---

5 Kevin Gilmartin, *Emotional Survival for Law Enforcement*, (Tuscon, Arizona: E-S Press, 2002) pages 89-90.

Faye has implemented the pause moment. She'll ask her husband how his day was and pause for the signs she's come to recognize after thirteen years on the force. Sometimes he'll be fine. Other times she'll hear a heavy sigh, and so she'll remain silent. She knows that if he needs to call one of two fellow officers that something is bugging him and that he'll let her know in his time. She then adjusts to his response as appropriate.

Communication comes first—verbal and non-verbal. If he's bothered about something, maybe he needs a trip to the gym. Maybe he just needs to hold his baby daughter for a while in silence or wrestle loudly with his boys. Maybe he needs to watch TV for a couple of hours and relax. The rub comes when you have plans for the evening. Or it's tag-team time and it's your turn to go to work. This happens over and over through the year and beyond. It's learning to ebb and flow with the moment and having the awareness and self-control to deal with this process positively.

I want him to be on his game when he needs to be and, if he isn't to let me know so I can give some space and move on. But nine times out of ten, it's difficult to do. He doesn't know what's on his mind; he's just irritable. Or he doesn't have the energy to articulate his needs. Sometimes he just lies on the bed and falls asleep. So much for dinner I spent time and energy making!

Brent has learned to be good about telling me when he is so spent he can't meet my expectations (at least the majority of the time). I have had to learn to be patient, and that right there is tough. Sometimes it just stinks! And I've decided that it's okay—for a season. When we understand that it isn't us, fight the temptation to panic or worry, and communicate like mature people, that's when it gets better. We develop thick skin. But it's keeping our hearts soft and bitterness-free over time that takes a bit more energy and focus.

I'm talking a lot about flexibility and allowing your officer to decompress from his job. But by no means am I suggesting we take a doormat mentality. We are an equal part of our marriages and have equal value. As cop spouses, we tend to be strong and sometimes outspoken, but not all of us. I'm suggesting ways to come alongside and support, but in the context of mutual love and respect for one another. There is a difference between being interdependent (the goal) and co-dependent.

After some years of trying to deal with hypervigilance and different moods, I learned I needed to communicate thoroughly. I had to initiate talk about the elephant in the room. I had to stand in front of the TV. Life shouldn't revolve around our spouse's career—but a lot of times it's unavoidable. It does affect our lives together, as I mentioned in chapter one. I had to find my voice—and had to learn to use it wisely when things were out of balance.

Achieving balance is how we create our normal. When Brent took over command of the CHP Academy, we were mentally prepared that it would take a lot of out of us. He worked long hours and maneuvered a large staff through some seemingly impossible demands. At times it was downright overwhelming. During these times he'd come home, share a bit with me, and we'd sit together, shaking our heads.

I wish I could share that we took advantage of his vacation time and gave him the down time he needed. But that wasn't the case. He actually built so much time up that he exceeded his vacation time limits. And we suffered as a couple and as a family. It has been one of the hardest seasons to go through in his career.

After two years of long days and many weekends, Brent wanted to umpire baseball games. I reluctantly agreed. It seemed at first like it was just more time away from our family. But when I saw the camaraderie he built with other guys and how happy he was when he returned, I didn't mind that he was gone the extra hours. I finally saw him relax. It became his replenishment; something he desperately needed.

During this time at the academy, my life was busy as well. He was busy with his job, and I was busy with my own pursuits. But one thing I did during this time was be available to listen when he came home. For much of our marriage, my guy didn't talk much about work. He usually had a lengthy commute to calm down from his shift. But as the academy commander, he entered the house, still talking on his phone. Because he couldn't talk with others about his frustrations, he vented to me. I was safe. I listened. I didn't say much—didn't need to. Sometimes I offered my female intuition, and he was pleasantly surprised that I could be so business smart. I liked that. It brought a new level of trust and respect to our relationship. All I had to do was be ready to close my mouth and open my ears.

The Hero at Home

Because this book covers different aspects of law enforcement marriage, it probably seems like my entire existence revolves around the fact that he is a cop. It doesn't. There are areas of our lives that have nothing whatsoever to do with law enforcement. This is a big question for new officers' wives. "I have my own job; do I have to drop everything for this to work?" The answer is no. Life is life. Kids. Careers. Hobbies. Church. Clubs. Sports. There is more to life than law enforcement.

Erica doesn't view her husband as a hero when he walks in the door. He's Marlo, the father of her children, the man she married, and the one who takes out the trash. So when he comes home, she expects him to jump into their lives. I love this. Erica has two boys and a career. She basically runs the home and likens it to a revolving machine. When Marlo comes home from his shift, she expects him to join their lives that are already in motion. Because she has communicated this, it works!

What you don't know about Erica is she had to face that horrible moment that we all fear: "Honey, I need you to come the hospital. I've just been shot!" Marlo called her from his stretcher on the side of the freeway. After this critical incident, she had to make things click in her mind. This was when she adopted this attitude: Marlo is the man she married. He's not Marlo the hero; he's Marlo the husband. He's Marlo the dad. In fact, she's only seen Officer Marlo a few times.

This mindset may be more difficult for others. When they are on duty, they have to take control in the midst of chaos. Your officer has been trained to be in control of situations and will be direct and to the point. He doesn't do multiple-choice on duty. What happens when he comes home, still in this attitude of control?

Mike, a retired police officer, told me once that he didn't know when he was being "a dick." Of course, I cried baloney! Other officers in the conversation came to his rescue, several nodding their heads. Jake said, "Hours on duty a day—our controlled, authoritative demeanor becomes second nature. I forget to turn it off when I go home." Really? This was news to me, but actually explained some things. Ben added, "Many times I'd come home with my cop talk and finally my wife answered back in the same tone. Took me by surprise! I realized at that moment, I'd been a jerk and didn't even see it."

That tone doesn't go over well. I know this might be easy for cops to forget to turn off, but it creates conflict at home, making spouses and kids feeling like criminals. The best course of action here is to remind them where they are, that words and tones have impact, and kindness matters. We can't suffer in silence, or fume inside with our indignation—it'll fester and come out in explosive spewing, or create a quiet bitterness that creates a wall almost impossible to tear down. This goes for spouses and kids alike.

Sometimes they'll come home and take charge. But we've been running things all day, and it's a little difficult to relinquish that position. We've got our tried and true ways of making it work, we understand the dynamics of what's going on, and then he comes in and tries to do things differently! Again, this is where respectful communication comes in. He needs to be a part of the home too, so don't hold on so tightly to your methods. On the other hand, you are not one of his customers, and he doesn't want you to be.

The other side of the spectrum is that they are tired of making decisions and/or babysitting crooks all day, and they don't want to take the reins at home at all. Recall the down stage of the hypervigilance roller coaster. It takes patient cooperation and respectful communication to find that balance, but it's worth the work.

The Long-term Perspective

I've mentioned several things that we see on a day-to-day basis—the short term. But there is a long-term perspective as well. In a career that spans twenty to thirty years, these issues will ebb and flow with the seasons. Supervisors and commanders come and go, and, depending on their leadership skills or lack thereof, your husband's career will benefit or suffer. Critical incidents, morale at the department, line of duty deaths and injuries, and even the anti-police rhetoric that plagues our streets and airwaves have an affect on our lives with our officers.

There have been seasons that Brent couldn't wait to get to work. And there were times when his stress was so elevated his blood pressure would reflect it. The point here is that seasons come and go. Things change often, sometimes for the better, sometimes for the worst. It's called life! We have to enjoy the good times when they come and endure/ embrace the rough spots for the character building they can instill. Either way, sometimes it just helps to know that it won't stay the same forever.

His Coping Mechanisms

Your cop will have his ways to deal with stress of the job. Some are destructive, which I'll talk about at length in chapter eight. Some coping mechanisms are fine, but you may not be crazy about them. A couple of years ago, Brent had a chief who dealt with stress by having an occasional outdoor cigar-smoking session with a few guys in the office. My daughters hated this. They always knew when Daddy smoked a cigar that day. But I knew that a few cigars over a several month period were unlikely to do any damage. In fact, it did him some good to take an occasional time-out in the middle of a hard workday.

Debriefing with their colleagues seems to help officers deal with stuff a bit easier. Suggest he play racquetball or golf or bike with some buddies. Maybe a yearly hunting trip is in order, or have him spend a morning fishing with a friend. During these times, it'll also help your attitude if you schedule something for yourself.

Cop humor, silence, Monday-night football, motorcycle riding, exercise…our officers need outlets. There has to be some way for them to de-stress. He's putting out a lot of himself to be an officer. You can help by listening, taking care of your portion of the marriage partnership, initiating sex, and creating a safe home. But as awesome as you are, you are not the only place he can be filled. Support an outlet or two that builds him up.

Our Response

Understanding our officers—who they are, what they do, how they deal with it—helps us to know better how to support them as life partners. But this is only half of it. How we respond is the other half.

Erica, whom I referred to earlier in this chapter, says that she doesn't think about police stuff each and every day he walks out the door. I don't either. But I suggest thinking through it when all is well, letting these thoughts digest so that day to day and year to year we grow and learn together instead of moving apart. In some ways, it's putting on our own mind armor to keep us in the marriage game as well.

We have a choice. We can begrudge the way they are and build a wall to protect our sense of who we think they should be (or in some cases, who they *used* to be). We could, over time, harden our hearts toward parts of them and complain behind their backs to our friends. We could demand that they change, and they might even try out of love for us. But, in the end, demands for change and resentment won't build up a marriage—it'll tear it to pieces.

Or we can accept them for who and what they are, respecting their processes. We can love them wholeheartedly for who they are and be forgiving for what they aren't. This acceptance gives them the freedom to be real. And in the security that this provides, they might even just mellow out over time. I've witnessed this in many marriages. We might say, "She's been good for him." At the very least they will appreciate the safe place that our love creates and trust us with depths of themselves we will treasure. Sex will be better, too, as the walls of mistrust disappear and we grow in intimacy.

On its surface, it seems like an easy choice. But it isn't. Marriage is hard. Marriage to a cop is even harder. How can we get the courage necessary to thrive amidst all of this?

<hr />

Discussion Group Questions

1. How does your officer wind down/relax from his workday? Do you feel this is working for him, you, and your kids?
2. Do you recognize symptoms of the hypervigilance rollercoaster in your officer? Elaborate.
3. What is an attitude that you feel you need to tweak that will improve your relationship with your officer?
4. Do you think you need to find your voice? If so, what specific area do you need to address with your officer?

CHAPTER 5
Thick Skin, Soft Heart: How to Deal Emotionally

*I don't wear the badge on a uniform. But
when you're married to an officer, you wear
the shadow of their badge on your heart.*
PAT, CALIFORNIA

*The job can be so consuming. But it's only part of
your life, not all of your life. You have an identity too.
Nurture your own career, kids, hobbies, or all of the
above. You can be supportive of your spouse while still
prioritizing the other things that make you whole.*
RACHEL, CALIFORNIA

*Worrying is carrying tomorrow's load with today's
strength—carrying two days at once. It is moving
into tomorrow ahead of time. Worry does not empty
tomorrow of its sorrow, it empties today of its strength.*
CORRIE TEN BOOM, HOLOCAUST SURVIVOR

A highway patrolman responded to an accident that involved a disturbed young man. One thing led to another, and a fight ensued as the man tried to steal the officer's gun. A sheriff's deputy joined in, as did a paramedic who was on the scene. The subject was overpowered, and he went to jail. This kind of thing happens often, but this time a reporter with a camera just happened to stop and snap several pictures of the entire incident. The photos made their way to a variety of places, and *Code 3 Magazine* picked them up and published them.

In response, they received an emotional letter from a wife of a police officer with three small children. She wrote that she was shocked to see such graphic pictures and didn't wish to receive the magazine anymore. In the next issue, there were several responses to her letter. Here are two excerpts:

> ...[B]elieve in your husband...and support him with all your heart. It is for you, your children and the world they live in that he serves as a peace officer. You are and need to be a part of that. A loved one's support and faith is often the secret weapon that a peace officer will use to survive a critical incident. Hiding from reality will not work.
>
> DEPUTY SHERIFF MARRIED TO A HIGHWAY PATROLMAN

> Being an officer's spouse is not for the faint of heart. It takes strength, will and an understanding for the love of the job that officers feel and commit themselves to... I hope she can come to terms with that which she is now married to. If not, her constant fear will destroy both her and her marriage...
>
> FORMER OFFICER AND WIFE OF POLICE OFFICER[3]

Fear had taken its toll on this young mother, and it seemed that she responded with avoidance and anger. It's a natural instinct but one that could be destructive to her and her family.

So, what's a spouse to do with the negative emotions? When we're struggling with what our officers do and the life we now live under the influence of a police career, or we're just plain weary of the demands of being an LEOW, how can we thrive in our marriages?

I interact with many families that are new to law enforcement. Many are filled with worry, afraid of the changes to come, and some just don't want it.

There are choices—1) leave, 2) stay and complain, 3) stay and ignore that your spouse is a cop, or 4) stay and educate yourself, support, and back up your partner.

As for the first option, some gals just can't or won't do it—and they opt out, like my friend in chapter one. The second option, complaining, is guaranteed to drive a wedge between you and your officer. Putting yourself in competition with their calling may actually find you in last place.

As for the third option, it is perilous. Kari chose to ignore policing for years because she resented the fact that her husband changed careers shortly after they were married. She almost lost her marriage. The road back was long and painful, but she decided to embrace him—and that meant she had to embrace his career. She actually went on a ride-along, and that really helped her perspective and understanding.

The fourth option is actually the best choice. Be open-minded at the beginning. If you're years into a law enforcement marriage, make a change in your heart to be more open and inquisitive. As negative emotions pop up, we can face them and work through them with a positive attitude. Easier said than done? Let's explore how.

Four Ways to Keep a Positive Attitude

The first way is to **stay educated**. Thirty years ago, cop wives were on our own to figure it out. Today, we have information at our fingertips. Ideas, tips, and perspectives—it's all waiting for us to read and experience. Don't know where to start? The resource section on our website—www.how2loveyourcop.com—is a great place! I've listed a variety of great books, websites, programs, and organizations for you to choose from. I try to keep it as current as possible, because there are new resources popping up all the time!

The second way is to **stay encouraged**. When the world is going crazy and they take it out on our officers, it is easy to get discouraged. When we're in one of those seasons of disconnect with our spouse, it's easy to get discouraged. When life gets complicated with work or kids or friends or all of the above, it's easy to let discouragement become our new norm.

I've been there. At one point, I considered giving up How2LoveYourCop because of discouragement. Voicing my feelings and considerations helped me realize I didn't have the full picture. My family and friends had much different perspectives—and they added missing information. In response, I surrounded myself with others—because listening to myself was only part of the story.

Which brings me to the third way to keep positive—**stay connected**. You and I need each other, pure and simple. From our place in the world, we see a lot. But we can't see everything. We can't know everything. And from time to time, our view is incomplete and even a bit distorted. A friend once said to me, "You don't find clarity alone." That is so wise! Isolation is a true enemy. Connect with others. Listen. Believe. Encourage.

The fourth way to maintain healthy perspective is to **stay engaged**. When we allow complacency to slip into our lives, we become vulnerable. Vulnerable to boredom, losing touch with our spouse, and other dangers. It is vital to stay engaged in our marriages—to pursue communication and cooperation, caring for each other regularly. If we are strong and stable, when the emergencies come, we are prepared. We have reserves stored up, and are not left with nothing. Operating from abundance has an effect on our attitude; it alone can be the difference.

When Martha's husband was let go by his department in the wake of a media-frenzied shooting, they were devastated financially, emotionally, and professionally—but not relationally. "We were strong together because we've always been strong," she told me. When everything blew apart, they had each other, and that is what sustained them. This marriage survived, and thrives to this day, because they had built a solid foundation.

Life, Liberty, and the Pursuit of Happiness

Worry and fear become chronic when the ground you stand on isn't firm enough to steady you. Every house is built upon a foundation, and the house will only be as sound as the materials it's built upon. If your personal foundation is built upon things like truth, morality, goodness, and a love for others, chances are you're standing on something solid that will withstand the storms life brings you. But if you are standing on ignorance, selfishness, fear of what could happen at any moment, or are led primarily by your senses (touch, sight, taste, etc.), your life will eventually falter on these shifting sands.

What is it that you stand on as an individual? What are your goals for your life? What drives you? When you are eighty years old, what do you want your life to look like as you take inventory of the years you invested?

The answers to these questions will determine your success in life as a person, a wife, a mother and levels of satisfaction or regret at the end of your life. It will also determine your emotional stability in the face of what your husband's career hands you.

Most women that I talk to want to be happy. That's what life is all about, right? We don't want trouble, and we don't want pain. We want to feel good inside and out, have fun, live positive lives with positive thinking. It's life, liberty, and the pursuit of happiness.

Unfortunately, if we are actively pursuing happiness, we are headed for disappointment, maybe even sorrow. Let me tell you why. Happiness is subjective. Happiness is elusive. And the definition of happiness is ever changing, depending on what it is that we chase to fill that happy place.

Years ago my youngest son wanted a Wii so bad he could taste it. He researched it on the web. He saved his money for months. Whenever we went shopping, he asked to swing by the electronics section just to see if they had them in stock. His pursuit of happiness was wrapped up in buying that Wii. Finally the day came when he received his Wii in the mail. For the next few weeks, he played Wii for hours. And, yes, he was so happy! But after a couple months, I noticed he was researching something else on the computer—catcher's gear. Here we go again!

Happiness is short lived. There will be times in your marriage that you will not be happy. There will be seasons that will take you down some dark paths. If your underlying pursuit is to be happy, you may want out in these seasons. Why? Because chasing a feeling that comes and goes will be a constant source of disappointment. And in that emotional instability, you will inadvertently undermine your own marriage.

Short-Term vs. Long-Term Thinking

Pursuing happiness is short-term thinking. It concentrates on right now. As I write this, I'd be very happy if I had a big piece of German chocolate cake. And then after I eat that very large piece of German chocolate cake, I'd be happy if I had just a little more. Fifteen minutes after eating another piece, I'll be miserable because my stomach hurts. And then in the morning when my jeans are too tight, the guilt sets in.

Long-term thinking is different. This mindset understands that passing on that dessert means better-fitting jeans, and that is the avenue to self-respect and good health. It is making a decision to pass on something that will make me happy temporarily to obtain something much more satisfying in the long run. Long-term thinking is realizing that when I am happy, I celebrate it because there will be seasons that I will not be happy. And yet I'm okay with it.

Long-term thinking in our marriages requires looking at the goal: to have a thriving marriage now and at the end of our lives. Actively pursuing a satisfying, contented marriage means investing in your relationship over the years in happy and not-so-happy times.

Long-term thinking doesn't blow things out of proportion when you have a spat this week after connecting on a deep level last week. Relationships ebb and flow, and short-term thinking will create drama. "You never..." is the accusation when, in actuality, he does at times just not enough for you or not enough at the moment. Drama gets tiresome when it pops up again and again. It takes out large withdrawals from your marital bank account. In contrast, long-term thinking relaxes a bit and doesn't panic. Long-term thinking stops taking cues from whatever doesn't feel right at the moment and tries to understand the big picture.

Put Fear in Its Place

The most common thing cops' wives hear from non-cops are questions about how we deal with fear. It's the first thing thought about once a loved one decides law enforcement is the career they want to do, and it's the most obvious. Those on the outside looking in assume that we worry all the time and the circumstances dictate to what degree. When Brent promoted to lieutenant and was relegated to a desk, our non-cop friends figured that I wouldn't worry as much because he was out of the danger zone. They were surprised to hear that I didn't worry as a lifestyle; that I had dealt with my fear long ago.

The first time I felt fear about my husband's job was about nine months in. He came home one morning and told me how he and his partner came upon a gang fight in a bad part of Los Angeles. Being the eager rookies they were, they stopped, called for back up, pulled their guns, and yelled freeze. And those who were fighting did freeze, unbelievably enough. All except for one, who took off. At that point Brent's partner gave chase, leaving Brent alone with over twenty gang members, having only a six-bullet revolver and a shotgun. It was at that point he realized that the situation could go really bad. They could've turned on him in a heartbeat...but they didn't.

It seemed like forever, but soon he heard distant sirens of the cavalry coming Code 3! Others arrived, black and whites screeching in from all directions. Gang members were sorted out, handcuffed, and taken to jail. Brent's partner came back too with the fleeing suspect in custody. Turns out, one of the bad guys was wanted for rape. It all turned out well, but the fear factor was definitely there.

Brent laughed about it—and at first, so did I. But it scared me. I started counting down the "what ifs," and fear crept in with them. Honey, we're not in Chico anymore! He's confronting real gangs with real guns. The danger was near, and it was very *real*.

At some point in your husband's career, you will face fear. Some of the wives I've talked to said the first year was the hardest, and then they settled down. Some of you have a natural tendency to worry, and this is hard for you. There are still others who hardly worry at all until they come face to face with a reminder that what their officers do *is* dangerous.

Rosa told me that she was having trouble with fear. Her husband had graduated from the academy just three months earlier and then was sent to Oakland. I understood; in that month there were two separate shooting incidents with our department alone and a riot deployment. A year earlier Oakland Police Department lost four officers to a single shooter. It was a dangerous place. She wondered how to deal with it.

When fear rears its ugly head, how can we deal with it? I think the answer lies in what we choose to put our faith in. What is it that we can hold on to that will be adequate to stand up to the "what ifs?" Let's look at a few facts—they're in our favor.

What are the facts surrounding line-of-duty deaths for American law enforcement officers? First, there are far fewer today than when line of duty deaths reached 280 in 1974. For the five most recent years preceding the reissuance of this book, an average of 134 officers died in the line of duty. Second, there are over 750,000 state and local law enforcement officers. Third, advances in training, tactics and equipment have reduced the risks. Listed below are the top ten causes of law enforcement death, with the annual average over the same five-year period:

1. Gunfire (46)
2. Automobile Accident (24)
3. Heart Attack (13)
4. Vehicular Assault (9)
5. 9/11 Related Illness (8)
6. Stuck by Vehicle (6)
7. Motorcycle Accident (5)
8. Vehicle Pursuit (5)
9. Duty Related Illness (2)
10. Gunfire (accidental) (2)

While gunfire is the leading cause, deaths have dropped from a high of 144 in the early 1970s to a third of that, again largely due to advances in training. What has also changed is the prevalence of social media. Forty years ago, news of an officer's death would be known locally, rarely an issue of national news. Today, each officer death is widely reported through social media. We feel the loss of each officer in a way that was not possible just a few years ago.

You'll notice on the list that two of the top three causes—automobile accident and heart attack—are areas that your officer can influence. Many spouses have saved their officer's life by insisting they wear their seat belt and watch their speed. Doing these two things has a substantial effect. As for heart attacks, getting an annual physical, exercising, reducing weight, and eating well are strategies to avoiding this cause. We can help with that, too.

There is a great deal of time, energy, thought, and money that goes into the training that your husband receives and continues to receive throughout his career. There are many people throughout the country whose jobs are to reduce the amount of injuries and deaths of police officers. Law enforcement training is designed to provide each officer the mindset, skill, and tactics to make it home at the end of each shift.

The same can be said about protective gear. There are constant innovations in body armor, tools, and weaponry. My husband receives catalogs and email every week that unveil the latest technologies available to law enforcement.

But we still lose excellent officers every year. It is a possibility no matter what the odds. So, how can we protect ourselves?

If something should go awry and you experience an injury or death, information is power; educate yourself. Here are several proactive steps you can take to ensure you are protected in these situations:

1. Do research on what your department provides for the families of fallen officers. In many cases, there may not be monetary benefits, but they might support you through assistance programs and help with funerals.
2. Know what federal and state benefits are available to you.
3. Make sure your husband's life insurance and accidental death/dismemberment is adequate for the needs of your family.
4. Draw up a will or living trust and provide a copy to the executor.
5. Keep your beneficiary information updated—too many benefits go to ex-wives and estranged family members. Make sure your children are included.
6. Ensure that your spouse keeps your contact information updated in the records at work (i.e., new address, phone numbers). This includes who he would want to make the death notification to you.
7. Have a conversation with your spouse about final wishes, how he wants to be buried and where, details he may want at his funeral, etc. If you can't do this, have him write it down and keep in a safe place.
8. Know that police survivors have a strong support community through Concerns of Police Survivors (COPS). Their website has a wealth of information, and should you have to face this, this organization will be there to help.

Proactive Steps To Deal with Fear

We can know the odds and be prepared for the worst. But there are always those close calls and creepy little feelings that come up from time to time. How do we disarm them?

1. Face the worst-case scenario. Much of what we fear is unknown, and fear breeds worry. Think through your greatest fear and play it out in your mind as to how you will deal with it. Come up with an emergency response to the "what if."
2. Demystify the experience. Familiarize yourself with your agency's death benefits and protocol. Talk to your spouse about who you would want to deliver the news should something happen. Security is very important to us as women, and not knowing what will happen *if* can be a catalyst for worry. Brent's agency encourages officers to designate who will notify next of kin in case. You can be a part of that decision or work to initiate such a protocol in your husband's agency.
3. Resist the temptation to listen to scanners or dispatch applications on the Internet. This is not a response to facing the worst-case scenario. This is a distracting illusion of control. "If I just know what's going on, I can handle it..." Risky approach. This could perpetuate fear, not dispel it.
4. Talk out your fears. I talked with Brent in his down time once or twice and found it helpful. I've also talked with other seasoned wives, and this helps too. You may even consider talking with a survivor if you have the opportunity. If you are a person of faith, prayer is an excellent way to talk out your fears. Personally, this is where I found much comfort when I have dealt with occasional fear.
5. Let it go. This is one area you can't control, and if you try you'll drive yourself and others crazy. Go back to your foundation. What or who is it that you trust?

Take a look at what fear really is. It is an unpleasant emotion caused by the belief that someone or something is dangerous, and likely to cause pain or threat. It isn't actually based on reality. I found a great quote by Will Smith from the movie *After Earth* that describes this well:

The only place that fear can exist is in our thoughts of the future. It is a product of our imagination, causing us to fear things that do not at present and may not ever exist. That is near insanity. Do not misunderstand me, danger is very real, but fear is a choice.

In contrast, faith is described as "the assurance of things hoped for, the evidence of things not seen."[6] We have a choice to choose faith or fear. We fight fear with faith.

My friend Michelle Walker lost her husband in the line of duty New Year's Eve of 2005. I asked her how she dealt with fear before he was killed. I learned that her father was with LAPD and had suffered a shooting but recovered. Incredibly, she never feared that her husband would be killed. She answered, "Fear drains your energy, puts stress on your marriage and family, and ultimately won't change a thing. I'm so glad that I didn't waste the time I had with Mike worrying."

When I Moved In, I Brought My Baggage

Jim and Angie sat across from us, their meals barely touched. They recounted an issue that they couldn't get past in their marriage, and it was huge. They were so concerned that they brought it to Brent and I, their mentors, to help them sort it out. About that time Brent asked, "Is this something that you struggled with in your home life growing up?" Jim's face froze, and I could almost see the light bulb brighten above his head. He then recalled a story that had paralleled their issue to the tee. The core issue was apparent to each one of us, and they came up with a simple way to deal with it.

In this life journey you've been on, chances are you have picked up things along the way that aren't so good. Someone hurt you. You have adopted others' destructive messages about yourself. Perhaps you made poor choices in your past, and you are reaping the consequences now. Whatever the reason for the hurts in your life, if not dealt with, they can adversely affect your marriage.

Dr. Gil Stieglitz, in his book *Marital Intelligence—A Foolproof Guide to Saving and Strengthening Marriage*, says that past baggage is one of five problems we face in marriage. He writes,

> *We carry with us wounds and destructive internalized programming as well as guilt and consequences from our past actions.*

---

6 Hebrews 11:1, KJV

There is no way to seal off the past and have its unresolved issues stay away. At times the impact of unresolved past baggage is so strong that it must be dealt with before progress in marriage can be attempted... It will continue as is unless those wounds are exposed, grieved, and processed... People need to process their pain from the past.[7]

Many are the hurts of those we know. Some heal, some don't. Some make peace with their pain; others live in the past. If baggage is affecting your relationship, there are healthy ways to deal with it. Check your support system (see chapter nine). Some things can be talked out with a wise friend. I also recommend meeting with an older, wiser couple with your husband. When Brent and I went through a tough time with one of our teenagers, we sought out the help of a couple we respected who'd gone through similar things with their son. It was a great help.

Counseling is also a great tool. I once heard a police officer say that when she needed help with plumbing she called a plumber. When she needed help with electrical, she called an electrician. So it only made sense when she needed help with some emotional issues she was facing, she called a therapist.

You have value. Who you are and what you contribute makes a difference in the lives of those close to you. You have strengths, and you have weaknesses. You don't have to be great at everything to be valuable to your marriage and family. If you feel like you do, you are carrying unrealistic expectations. But you are good at some things—concentrate on those strengths and use them for your benefit and that of your family.

The Whole You

I've talked about motivation, foundations, problems, and trust. These are some deep parts of yourself you may never have thought about in this context. But I come back to them because it is so important to know who you are. When we know who we are, then we are much better equipped to deal with whatever life hands us. We know what will work and what won't. It's much better than going through life just guessing.

---

7 Gil Stieglitz, *Marital Intelligence*, (Winona Lake, IN: BMH books, 2010) page 184.

When Brent went into the academy to become a highway patrolman, I went through my own transformation at home (the CHP Academy is a six-month live-in arrangement with most weekends off). I had to stand on my own two feet for the first time in my life. I had a home to run, a job to perform, and on the weekends a husband to encourage and support. Back in the day before e-mail and cell phones, I had no way to get in touch with him during the week. I had to rely on his ability to use the one phone on campus while completing rigorous eighteen-hour days. He didn't call much, and I missed him terribly.

It was during this time that I discovered that my husband would not meet all of my needs. Fulfillment could not be found in him alone, nor could he secure my insecurities. This was hard to accept; I came into our marriage with an expectation that he would do all that. I did some soul-searching, found a mentor, and grew up a little. It was a good thing too because that toughened me up for our first assignment in Los Angeles.

The best approach to our relationship with our husbands is as whole people. They can meet some of our needs but not all. Spending some time answering the motivation and foundation questions is a good start. Learning to communicate is the next step.

Group Discussion Questions

1. When you are eighty years old, what do you want your life to look like as you take inventory of the years you invested?
2. Do you struggle with fear and/or worry? If yes, what is something you're willing to try to combat it? If you don't struggle with fear, share with others your thoughts about why, or how you've gotten to that place.
3. How would you describe your attitude towards your spouse being an officer?
4. What is one way you incorporate either short-term or long-term thinking?

CHAPTER 6

SPEAKING IN CODE: COMMUNICATION

*Listen when they want to share. Their stories are crazy,
fun, scary, hilarious and so much more. But don't be
afraid to let them know a story was too much or makes
you nervous about the job. When he doesn't want to talk
about it, don't push. When they are ready they will share.*

JENNIFER, CALIFORNIA

*Don't take anything personally, have someone
on the outside to be a sounding board, have ten
more on the inside to be a support system...*

SARAH, PENNSYLVANIA

A sleek, black Lexus caught my eye in the next lane. Wow. It was shiny
and new, and the sun hit it just right. It's a good thing I noticed it
because all of a sudden it cut me off! So I'm driving behind this gorgeous car, and I veered into the left turning lane (with my signal on).
Again, this Lexus cut me off to do the same (but without a signal). What?!
Am I supposed to know where he's going?!

As we both made the left turn, he braked hard and made a quick right
into a gas station, once again with no signal. Because I'd kept my distance
for my own car's sake, it wasn't dramatic, but it made me mad. Such a
beautiful vehicle but the driver was clueless!

I call this "driving on the inside of the car," and it's one of my biggest
pet peeves. There are many of these people on the road—those who

don't think to let others know what they're doing by flipping a simple switch. (Actually, when I think about it, it really shouldn't bug me. It is, after all, job security for my husband! But I digress…)

It's called a failure to communicate. And it doesn't just happen on the road. It happens in relationships every day. Someone is acting on the thoughts inside her head, and she expects others to be able to understand exactly what she's doing and why. But if she doesn't give out the proper signals, she runs the risk of making someone angry or, worse, causing damage to herself and others.

Lost in Translation

Communication can be so tricky at times. Words come from deep within a person's soul and heart. They come with a set of values, experiences, and personal makeup. On the other end, the same words are received into a new set of values, experiences, and different personal makeup. At times I speak a different language from my husband. I can speak a different language from my kids, my mother-in-law, or fill in the blank.

Much of our communication gets lost in translation. If good communication is critical for a lasting relationship, how can we learn to speak each other's language?

The most obvious way is to spend time with each other. That's a no brainer. But what about when things change, like when a child is born or a critical incident occurs? What about when time goes by, you lose touch, and suddenly you are clueless to what's going on with your husband?

Colorful Personalities

Brent and I had reached a point in our marriage where we were in a rut, struggling to understand each other. We were clashing, not in sync, and we were both frustrated. Then Brent brought home a book called *The Delicate Art of Dancing with Porcupines*, by Bob Phillips. This book is based on four types of people— the analytical, the driver, the expressive, and the amiable— and explores how these people interact and communicate.[8] We answered the questions in the book and were amazed at the results.

When I understood the natural tendencies of my husband, it was a huge "aha" moment and vice versa. We spent a couple of hours laughing over each other's tendencies and how we differ. It gave us freedom to be ourselves and a non-threatening way to give each other the freedom to be who we are. It was a huge step toward understanding each other, and our relationship has only gotten better because of it. When we come to a situation from two different sides, we are able to see where each other is coming from and then come to a better solution for both.

We also learned about a similar program through our church that was adapted from several sources. This tool categorizes people into colors based on personalities. Red people love fun and are very talkative. Blue people tend to be caretakers, romantic, cooperative, and peacemakers. Green people are problem solvers, leaders, and logical in their thinking. Yellow people are planners, punctual, and structured. We became more self-aware and learned how our colors respond to each other.

Brent is a green, and I am a blue-red combo. Bring our kids into the mix and we have all four colors represented. In moments of peace, we all actually talk about what colors we are. It helps to understand why we do what we do and react how we react. It is a valuable tool to step outside of ourselves and see each other with different eyes.

The Man-Woman Thing

I like to joke that when God took a rib from Adam to make Eve, He took a whole lot more than just a bone. He also took the multitasking gene, the tendency to nurture, and the ability to ask for directions! But seriously, not only do we deal with our differences in personalities, we also have the man-woman thing.

So many people are irritated with the obvious differences between males and females. I've seen a lot of women try to change their guys, make an attempt to get them in touch with their feminine side. Men seem to either joke or just shake their heads at female tendencies. It is almost

---

8 Bob Phillips, *The Delicate Art of Dancing with Porcupines*, (Ventura, CA: Regal Books, 1989) page 43.

impossible to truly understand the inner workings of the opposite sex. It's a fact: we are different, and neither is more important than the other. So how can we live together in harmony?

I say let's accept the differences and learn to appreciate them. Be who you are as a woman. Let him be who he is as a man. Accept the fact that he can't say as many words as you do in a day and find other outlets (like other females) for the rest of your important thoughts and ideas. Celebrate his ability to be firm with the kids when you waver, and celebrate that you want to hug your little sweetie for as long as she needs. Understand that the best way to talk to your guy is when you do something together. Women like to talk face to face, but men talk best side by side.

We were made to work together. Like a key fits into a lock, our physical anatomy is definitely suited to each other. But it doesn't end with anatomy. Our personality traits, strengths, and natural tendencies are so different it seems for some that we could never be compatible. But with the right attitude and enough time, you and your spouse can learn to ebb and flow with each other's strengths and weaknesses. It is a beautiful thing to behold a couple with this kind of balance.

Love Languages

"I just don't feel loved by my husband..." I have heard this from many women throughout the years. Usually her husband actually loves her deeply but isn't able to show her in the way she can receive it. This too is about speaking a different language. In Gary Chapman's book *The 5 Love Languages: The Secret to Love that Lasts*, he describes five ways in which people feel loved. They are quality time, gifts, words of affirmation, physical touch, and acts of service. Each person has at least one of these ways they feel loved, and they tend to show love this way as well. A problem arises when both spouses have different love languages. More often than not, this is the case.

Say that Sue's love language is words of affirmation, and Raymond's is acts of service. Sue will naturally tell Raymond she loves him often, but he would feel more loved if she offered to take his uniforms to the dry cleaners. Raymond will show Sue he loves her by washing her car, but she wants to hear how he loves her and why. Do you get the rub?

Just knowing how to speak each other's love language can improve your communication dramatically. It takes a choice on two fronts: choose to show love in his language, and recognize his love language toward you and appreciate it. Better yet, get proactive; talk about love languages together and use the knowledge to love each other more effectively.

A Sixth Love Language

"I don't think my husband shows or feels love in these ways. There is a sixth love language," asserted Sarah.

I have a friend who keeps me on my toes. Sarah comes up with thought-provoking ideas and will come at me with a smirky smile, piercing eyes and her armor on.

"Okay, Sarah, what is the sixth love language?"

She described a sort of sarcasm that isn't designed to wound. The words are strong, maybe a little harsh, but they're backed with connection. It's a way of communicating with a smirk and a twinkle that is shocking, yet affectionate. The interaction asks if you brave enough to handle the unvarnished truth, or safe enough to accept my criticism. It's a challenge to step into the ring and tease each other until we're friends.

My thoughts went to my father-in-law (former cop) who communicates this way. If you can't handle the verbal spar, he doesn't respect you. I thought of several co-workers of my husband, and a Vietnam Vet whom I dabbled in the ring with at a book function, and especially my co-author of *Selfish Prayer*—he is the champion of verbal spar.

Sound like anyone you know?

Once I spoke to 30 middle management police officers in Oakland. Most people would feel uncomfortable talking to a group who sat in a U-shape, dressed in their uniforms with bars and stripes gleaming from the fluorescent lights above. They sat stone-faced, wheels turning, some making a few notes as I spoke about what I offer police marriages. I spoke in my normal encouraging way, speaking passionately about my cause. One of them interjected. "Got anything in that book of yours that deals with cops that want to sleep with married cops? Cause that's what I'm dealing with right now."

Here we go.

I replied yes, I do mention this briefly in my book, and then said something like, "That's why I do what I do. It may be kind of Pollyanna, but perhaps if we can strengthen marriages, you won't have to deal with it on duty."

They weren't convinced. So I switched to the sixth love language.

"Look, we do what we can, but sometimes shit happens..."

The entire room erupted into laughter. I was suddenly one of the club. Believe it or not, I felt trusted. I'd made the connection. Not by speaking my language, but *theirs*.

I truly believe there is a sixth love language. It is a language of love and trust spoken by men and women who deal with the painful realities of our world—cops, military, search and rescue, firemen, medical personnel. Probably others, too.

Verbal sparring is a tough language to speak because it dances close to uncomfortable. It sometimes draws blood. I wondered if it was actually a language of love, or just a way to be a jerk. My conclusion is that it is a different way of loving and communicating love that is safe in a life that demands tough talk, tough skin, in tough times.

Communication Killers and Keepers

Learning to speak each other's language is a lifelong pursuit. It's the big picture, a little something to keep in the back of your mind year to year. But what about day to day? That's where the bulk of our communication lies.

There are behaviors and mindsets that will kill the ability to communicate, and there are attitudes and boundaries that will keep the communication flowing. Brent and I call them communication killers and keepers. In the following pages, I explain each killer and it's opposing keeper.

Unspoken Expectations vs. No Givens

If you want to learn each other's language, you have to *speak*. So much of miscommunication is unspoken. We develop assumptions based on our own personal views and values. We have assumptions about how relationships operate, how they should be, and then these assumptions turn into expectations. But when those expectations are not talked about, there's conflict.

I was brought up in a home that taught if you weren't fifteen minutes early, you were late. Brent was brought up in a home where perpetual lateness was the norm. This became a huge issue for us, especially because of the nature of his crisis-driven career. I was offended and frustrated time after time because we could never get anywhere when I wanted to be there. After many discussions and tearful arguments, we learned to talk about the expectations each other had about time management.

Newlyweds Mark and Rachel had guests over for the evening. The weekend before, Rachel spent extra time cleaning the house, and she planted flowers in the backyard. Then she took off work early and prepared an appetizer to go with the drinks, made up the meal ahead of time, and put together a beautiful dessert. While the guests were there, Mark offered up some drinks and talked with the guys while he grilled the meat. All had a great evening with lots of laughs. Once the guests had gone, Mark declared he was exhausted and that he had to get up early for the day shift. He promptly went to bed. Rachel, who also had work the next morning, stayed up late cleaning up after everyone, fuming. She didn't talk to Mark for two days.

Before you get too angry with Mark, you must understand something. His mother was a stay-at-home mom who did *everything* for her family. She cooked dinner every night and cleaned up afterward without batting an eye. He had absolutely no clue how much work goes into entertaining, much less thoughts about helping to clean up. His unspoken expectation was that Rachel would handle it. Rachel, on the other hand, neglected to voice her expectation that he help with clean up because she assumed he would. His ignorance and her anger were both a result of unspoken expectations that neither of them were aware of.

Expectations do not kill communication; failing to express them does.

Mark and Rachel would have had a much different outcome had they taken a few minutes to discuss each other's responsibilities beforehand. It wouldn't have been much for him to clear the table and load the dishwasher while she rinsed. The whole evening was a success until Rachel was offended by her own assumptions.

Take the time to understand expectations for events, your job, even day-to-day things. Then negotiate solutions to those expectations. There are no givens!

Unforgiveness vs. Keeping Short Account

When our unspoken expectations are not met, it is very easy to develop resentment. We take it personally. But that really isn't fair, is it? How can our husbands know they did something wrong if they don't know the rules?

Years ago when Brent was working swing shift, he'd normally get off around midnight. One night in particular, he called me from the office to say that he had to write some reports and wouldn't be home for a while. About 2:30 a.m., I woke up and discovered he wasn't there yet. I called the office. They told me he'd left about a half hour earlier. Because I assumed he'd be there any minute, I waited up for him.

In the meantime Brent stopped to fuel up on the way home and struck up a conversation with the gas attendant. They had a very deep, meaningful conversation that lasted about two hours. By the time Brent drove up, I was convinced he was dead and then decided he was having an affair. Either way he would need a funeral! And, of course, I'd planned it all out.

After I unleashed my full fury on him, he told me what happened. He apologized, and I forgave him. Now we laugh about the string of obscenities that flowed from my mouth when I rarely cuss. And that is that.

Unforgiveness will not only kill communication, it will kill your relationship and could eventually kill your soul. No matter how you look at it, you lose. The thing that will keep communication flowing is keeping a short account. Let the anger go.

Brent calls this the emotional bank account. When we spend time together, do favors for each other, have good sex, etc., we are making deposits into the relationship. Arguments, harsh words, unspoken or demanding expectations, slamming doors, etc., are withdrawals from your relationship. Just like money, you look at your account at the end of each month, and hopefully your account is in the black. But too many withdrawals will cause it to fall into the red.

The currency of your relationship isn't cash; it's trust. When there isn't enough give for the take, you run into problems. When Brent was unaccounted for late into the night, fear consumed me. It was a big withdrawal. But when we decided he would phone home if a situation like this came up again (and it did), we made a deposit into our account. When I decided to let it go by forgiving him, we were in the black again. He learned from it too and never made that type of mistake again.

Unkindness vs. Setting Speech Boundaries

As a law enforcement family, there will always be pressures as we looked at in the first chapter. Unfortunately the easiest place to release that pressure is on those closest to us. And the closer you get, the worse it can be. Because we are so entwined, when our spouses go through stuff, it affects us and vice versa.

Earlier I mentioned a brush that went flying through the air at Brent on Christmas morning. The pressures at that moment were very great; we were newlyweds, we just moved, we didn't know anyone, we didn't have any money, and he was dealing with people on the road for the first time—it was nuts. That pressure really built up in me, and then when we fought Christmas morning, look out! She's gonna blow! And blow I did.

But it doesn't always go that way. What about when we're irritated with each other, or the kids, or the neighbor's dog that kept us up all night? Unkindness has a way of creeping in. We start treating each other poorly. Little digs here and there, our voices raise a bit, our patience wears thin. It gets old quick.

After our argument on Christmas morning, Brent and I settled down enough to decide that we needed to implement some ground rules. Here's what we came up with:

The first thing we decided was to never use divorce as a threat. We have friends who do, but we decided that this was too big of a withdrawal for us both. Brent's parents divorced when he was young, so divorce is painful for him. I came into our relationship with trust issues caused by philandering ex-boyfriends. We chose to treat this topic as taboo. The commitment that we made has helped us to do this. We *never* go there.

Second, we don't use sarcasm. When there are unresolved conflicts in a relationship, sarcasm is easy to muster. But it is also a cowardly way to throw insults. Someone says something mean and then laughs it off as a joke. It's not a joke. It hurts just as much. And usually sarcasm is used when other people are around. Let me just say if you use sarcasm against your spouse in front of other people, you just created an embarrassing situation and cast a shadow on your own character. They'll think you're a jerk whether you are or not.

The third boundary we set is that we will never insult each other. This includes name-calling, comparing with other people, and just being mean.

This doesn't mean that we don't joke or tease. But jokes and teasing are not meant to cut someone down but rather to lighten up. In fact humor is an excellent way to release some pressure.

One last thing. Something that comes really easy to us women is nagging. Many times our guys don't get things done in a timely manner whether it's because they tend to procrastinate or their schedules just don't allow for it. Either way, nagging is destructive. It won't get us what we're hoping for, which is action. Because my husband's job is so high velocity, he needs down time on the weekends and time with our kids. Weeks will go by with his honey-do list untouched. I am so tempted to nag, nag, and nag some more!

But over the years I have learned to combat this urge with these two ideas:

1. I'll ask supportive questions like "I know you've been working so hard lately. Is there anything I can do to help you get this done?" Many times there is a reason he can't get it done. Perhaps he has to research how to do it, or the hardware store didn't have the right part. Many times I might be able to help him get past the obstacle, and then it gets done.
2. I tattle on him to my journal. It may seem a little silly, but it works. When I get to the point where I want to nag (or release frustration in other ways), I write it out and then throw it away. Actually, when I do this, it helps me work through the emotion so I can see the deeper issue. Then I'm in a much better position to communicate constructively.

Selfishness vs. Listen with the Desire To Understand

This last communication killer is so common it's actually part of our culture. We're encouraged to look out for ourselves, to be self-focused. We're also naturally inclined to respond to our own desires, feelings, and whims. We've been doing it since we could breathe. Maturity comes when you can keep your selfish tendencies in check, thinking and acting as if others are important too.

In a way your husband has sworn to the department that he will set selfishness aside; that he would lay down his life to save another. This is unselfishness at its best, real hero quality. You as his wife have agreed to share him for the greater good, another unselfish quality.

But in the day to day, we each have needs and wants that call to be met. We have dreams to pursue and goals to accomplish. So it's a dichotomy, making sure that we take care of ourselves but also tending to the needs of our husbands, kids, work, etc.

If we really want an outstanding relationship, we will make a choice to listen with a desire to understand each other. But it requires character—humility, even—to set ourselves aside for a time to truly listen.

Roger Williams, Director of the Mount Hermon Conference Center once said, "Selfish people will never live in unity." In marriage, everything needs to be filtered through *us*. Not "me," but "we." And the "we" includes us both—sometimes him, sometimes me, and sometimes both. There's a give and take here. And it takes practice.

Keep it Positive

One unfortunate thing that I have heard over and over again from the police community is that cop wives have a reputation for issues with their mouths. Gossip. Slander. Drama. Negativity. Complaining. Judging from some of the LEOW Facebook pages that I have decided not to follow, I'd say there is some truth to it. I've seen some posts that are repulsive. Mean. Foul. They spew hatred for others, and wow, is it ever ugly. Let me ask—is this what we want to be known for? Does this create open communication, trust, and community? Hardly. Trust me, I have my moments. I get angry just like anyone else. But over the years, I've learned to harness it—keep it under control. I've learned that there are ALWAYS two sides to a story, and once both sides are heard, judgment is a little harder to come to.

Our officers hear that negativity on the streets and in the office every shift. If they are coming home to it as well, there is no escaping, and that is so discouraging. We gotta give it a rest—leave the drama be, and keep positive in our approach to communication.

Good Communication Takes Time

I once heard a couple that had been married for over forty years say, "We didn't really get each other until we'd gotten the first twenty years out of the way." Now that Brent and I have been married almost 30, I understand what they were talking about. Molding two trees into one takes time and patience. It takes being lifelong students of one another. And as soon as you think you have him all figured out, he'll change. So will you. It's the adventure, and it's never dull!

This reminds me of good ol' Shrek and his conversation with Donkey. Shrek refers to himself as an onion. He has layers—really rough on the outside and soft and pliable on the inside. I can look back now and see that our marriage has been like this. We dealt with rough, unattractive stuff early on in our marriage, then, year after year, we've grown deeper and more pliable with each other.

Power Trip

This is a difficult chapter. Good communication requires responses that don't always come naturally. It takes courage and inner strength to speak the truth in a way that doesn't leave our partners wounded. But understand something, friends: you have power. You have the power to crush your spouse, to let your frustration fly in his face, or slowly, methodically undermine him. Either way, it could reduce him to shreds. The closer you grow, the more dangerous you become. You and I both know some women who are very good at this.

But you also have an opportunity to use your power to do something incredible. You have a choice to build him up into the man he deserves to be. Your love and respect can build strength and confidence in him.

You can strengthen that thin blue line, indirectly, through careful, proactive words and actions—words that encourage, even heal—actions that respect who he is.

—⊶⊷—

Discussion Group Questions

1. What is your love language? What is your husband's? How can you tell?
2. Name one unspoken expectation that has come up in your marriage.
3. What is one communication killer you deal with at home?

CHAPTER 7
WHEN TO STAND UP AND STAND DOWN: RESOLVING CONFLICT

Forgiveness and bitterness—without the first
you will limp through life with the second.
Forgiveness must occur if you ever hope to be
free of your painful past. It does NOT mean you
agree...it does mean you let it go forever!
CHUCK SWINDOLL[9]

Never leave without telling each other you love
each other and mean it. Tomorrow isn't promised.
NATALIE, OKLAHOMA

"We fight *all* the time," said Barry, a policeman from Virginia. His wife Marie nodded nervously. We stood together in the middle of a sea of peace officers, survivors, spouses, strollers, and others, waiting for the Candlelight Vigil to begin at the National Law Enforcement Memorial.

In the heart of Police Week, groups of officers descended upon Washington D.C., paying tribute to their fallen comrades, each in their own way. Some brought their spouses, eager to share the experience with their backup at home. This is why Barry and Marie were present.

We began to talk about their conflicts, giving them a different perspective of their arguments. Soon, Barry declared, "We need your book!"

---

9 Founder of Insight for Living, Pastor, Author, and Christian Educator

They looked at their disagreements as something negative. It scared them, made them wonder if they'd made a mistake in getting married. Understandable. But not true.

A New Attitude About Conflict

Conflict occurs when my motivations or ideas are at odds with my spouse's. Marriage brings together two individuals into one life together, and many of the goals, values, and ideas will not mesh immediately. We have two independent personalities that need to work together, depend upon one another, live and love together. This is interdependence.

Arguments are the hashing out of these differences. Conflicts are either barriers to interdependence, or bridges to intimacy. Our attitudes and choices determine which one it will be.

"Once I realized arguments were to move towards resolution instead of to be won, we started moving towards that goal," said Randy. "A cop will win every argument...we're trained to." We have to ask ourselves, "Am I seeking to understand my partner, or just standing my ground to get my own way?"

Before we were married, Brent and I had an argument. His perspective made sense, but I couldn't get my thoughts together to make a rebuttal. So I reverted to withdrawal and pouting. "OK, you're right. I'm wrong!" It was a move I'd done my whole life to avoid conflict, which was extremely uncomfortable for me. He wasn't buying it.

"How do I know that you're wrong? You're not talking to me," he reasoned. "I may *not* be right! You have to talk to me, so we can figure this out!"

Well, there's a concept! Squashing my opinions to avert an argument would not have resulted in *peaceful* resolution. I wanted the uncomfortable feelings between us to go away, but just because the argument ended didn't mean there was peace. The argument would have been replaced by self-pity. This is not peaceful by any stretch of the imagination.

I took him up on his challenge. We had the most mature conversation of my life to that point.

My way separated us—shut down communication and put up a wall of anger and bitterness. His way unified us—both have a say and thus arrive at a solution that benefits us both.

Growing up, I used to think that conflict was bad. I created a habit of shutting down my feelings to avoid conflict. Eventually I lost my ability to communicate, and then pity set in—I made myself a victim. When Brent gave me permission—a safe place—to argue my point, this empowered me to believe what I had to say was both valid and valuable. In the process I found my voice.

Conflict is a way to work towards deeper trust and intimacy. We have the opportunity to discover more about our officers and ourselves as we dissect the motivations and ideas we each have to offer. We have the opportunity to move past something together—to learn to cooperate. When we approach our conflicts this way, we build trust and understanding—the ingredients needed for mature, thriving relationships.

There's another benefit to conflict. When two minds tackle a problem, a different solution altogether has the chance to emerge. Not his way or her way, but our way. The discussion that two individuals contribute to has the potential to break through, change thinking in a positive way, and then something beautiful happens—clarity.

Expectations: Reasonable or Unreasonable?

If there is discord, misunderstanding or conflict, often it is because others failed to meet our expectations. They didn't make it on time, they didn't have the right response, they were insensitive, or they didn't do what was asked. We are disappointed, even angry. We want to lash out, and sometimes we want to give up. So much of failed expectations are based on assumptions. Is it possible your officer is failing to meet your expectations because they are not understood? Could it be the other way around?

Here are some questions that will help to expose expectations:

- What am I expecting of my spouse? My kids?
- People at work, school?
- What am I expecting of friends, family?
- What am I expecting of God?
- What do others expect of me?
- Are these expectations fair?
- Have I communicated them clearly?

We can't control the unexpected happenings of life, and obviously we won't always get what we expect. But we can take honest inventory of what we expect from those we love, and communicate clearly, improving our relationships, and making life just a little bit better.

Resolving Problems: Rules and Tools

Our officers solve problems for a living. They are constantly responding to conflict that has gotten out of control, or gone too far. They are trained to de-escalate conflict and have tools to keep them safe. In the spirit of what they do, I thought it would be fun to point out that some of those tools can be reminders of how to resolve our relational conflicts.

- **Flashlight**. Whether it's searching the interior of a house or looking at a suspect's eyes for signs of intoxication, the flashlight is indispensible. When we are in the midst of a conflict with our spouse, we need more information. We need more understanding so we can pinpoint the issue and then resolve it. Much conflict is caused by misunderstanding or unmet expectations. Get out the flashlight, so to speak, by asking questions that will bring light to the conflict.
- **Handcuffs**. When a suspect is taken into custody, he is cuffed to maximize his safety and that of our officers. When in a disagreement, resolve to make the conversation safe by remembering we're on each other's team. We are not adversaries, even if we're both passionate about our views. Use restraint and turn toward, not against; listen to understand.
- **Taser**. This tool stops a person in his tracks so officers can get him under control. When anger is out of control, stop it in its tracks by a soft answer. Acknowledge the anger, investigate why the anger is there, and then understand it.
- **Radio**. Dispatch speaks, they listen. If he talks over her, they miss what each other is saying. Both respond and vice-versa until they understand what needs to be done. When you are in the midst of an argument, do the same. You'll solve a lot more than speaking or yelling over one another.

Matt and Laura take walks together when they have disagreements. They used to fight the entire time and come home angry. Then Matt suggested they argue to the halfway point and resolve to come to resolution the rest of the way. The walk they took was four miles long. At two miles, there is a stop sign that they touch—a symbolic signal that it is time to stop arguing and come to a solution. This approach has been very helpful.

- **Ticket Book**. Although not carried on the duty belt, this tool is a reminder of a crucial ingredient to resolving conflict. Officers issue citations to record the violation. Likewise, we have to pinpoint where the problem lies—what is the violation? Have we wounded each other in some way? If so, an apology is needed. What can we do better next time? A little humility can bring peaceful resolution.

Somewhere in the course of our culture's *evolving* relational intelligence, we have adapted the thought that admitting our shortcomings will have a negative effect on our self-esteem and the respect others have for us. Newsflash—those we live with *already know* we aren't perfect. Understanding and acknowledging the stupid things we do makes us authentic and engenders respect.

When we admit our shortcomings, we take away their power over us. Rather than expend the energy to hide, deflect, and lie about the things we don't do well, or the wrong things we say, the mistakes we make, or whatever the case may be, we can use the energy to come clean. It's much less exhausting to be authentic than to keep up the lie.

There's an added bonus. When we give ourselves freedom to make peace with our weaknesses, we're much more willing to forgive others for their shortcomings. A willingness to come closer and connect emerges because there is permission to fail. I can be who I am—good, bad, and ugly—if there is mercy, forgiveness and restoration. (This doesn't extend to abuse, and it doesn't give license to chronic bad behaviors. Although, admitting a problem is the first step to restoration in such cases.)

Seasons of Marital Disillusionment

You meet someone who is a little different than everyone else. There's chemistry. Attraction. Camaraderie. You've found your life partner and take the plunge.

Your marriage begins with great joy, starting a life together in deep love that you are confident will never wane. Until disillusionment creeps in. The time of arrival of this unwelcome visitor varies. But at some point, you realize that things aren't exactly what you thought they'd be.

There was a shift. A difference. Unmet expectations. Arguments. And suddenly, marriage is hard. Disillusionment gives way to doubt. You find yourself questioning yourself, your spouse, and your future together.

A lot of marriages will hit this stage hard. They're surprised. There was no vision for what life would be like in the years after the wedding. The engagement was about the big day, the honeymoon, and then where to put all of the really awesome stuff you got. The excitement dies down, life goes back to normal, and then what? This is where the work starts—where the process of integrating two lives into one begins. And it isn't easy.

To get through the disillusionment stage, deeper understanding is needed. Whom did I marry? How are we going to live together amidst these conflicts? What do we want in our lives? What has changed? Why are we having so much trouble?

If you seek out the answers to these questions, you will find understanding. Understanding for your spouse. Understanding yourself more completely. Understanding how to live together, resolve differences, make compromises, and make changes that benefit you both. You then find yourselves knowing how to love each other just a little bit better. Your love begins to mature.

Falling In and Out of Love

When some couples hit the disillusionment stage, they assume that they've *fallen out of love*. We say that we fall in love with someone, as we find ourselves primarily intensely attracted to that person. This emotion is only one aspect of what committed, lifelong marital love is about.

Love is an action, not a feeling. Feelings flow from actions. You can't fall out of love. You can, however, choose to stop loving. Struggling or even miserable people sometimes go this way.

Love is about choices. We choose to move forward in our relationships. We choose to learn more about our spouses, and through what we learn, we gain the understanding to be a better lover.

The emotions that drew us together in the beginning may disappear for a time. But those emotions will return once we make a choice to actively understand, actively love.

When You're Miserable

If you and your spouse are in one of these seasons, there are some things to try before you file the papers. If there's anything in you that wants to fulfill the vow you made on your wedding day, you must recommit to the health and future of your marriage.

The first place you start is in your mind. Are you still in? If not, recommit yourself to your spouse again.

Second, look at your relationship objectively. You may not understand where your spouse is coming from, so start with you. What is it about the relationship that you can change?

I sat with Brendan as he told me his marriage was over. "I just need a reset. I don't like who we've become. I just want to start over."

"Obviously you don't want the marriage you've had up to this point," I countered. "But what if you could have a different marriage with the same person? A fresh start doesn't mean everything has to change—maybe just some things."

We have the ability to choose to do things differently. Brendan went back to his wife and they talked about the areas of their life together that they didn't like. They realized that a lot of it were things they could change, like where they lived, and habits they'd formed.

Third, choose to love as your duty. Go through the motions of acting like you love your spouse. The feelings will follow later. Time will give you clarity. When you're in crisis and there is hurt between you, there is a tendency to get caught up in the drama and make rash decisions.

Slow down. Let things ride for a while, giving you both a chance to listen, understand, and make reasonable decisions.

Finally, invest time and attention into your relationship. Attend a marriage retreat. See a therapist who understands law enforcement. Date once a week, or as often as you can. Ask questions with the intent to understand. Flirt with your spouse like you did when you first met. Renew or revamp your vision of who you want to be as a couple.

Attitude

If conflicts are to be resolved in a marriage, humility and respect are required. If both people in the relationship are to have equal value, we have to understand that there are two sides to every story. When your officer investigates an accident, he doesn't just ask one side. He talks to both drivers to get their perspective, interviews witnesses, and then looks at the physical evidence. When a disagreement arises, be open to the possibility that you may not perceive things correctly. Humility takes us there. To take on an attitude of humility, we choose to ask questions first instead of demanding our position. Humility teaches that our perspective is never perfect and acknowledges mistakes. Humility also softens the tone and slows down the disagreement, allowing for understanding.

Mutual respect is also crucial to conflict resolution. Much conflict is due to misunderstanding or miscommunication. When we respect each other, our thoughts are not poisoned by mistrust—we believe the best of each other. I value my spouse—therefore I want resolution.

Forgiveness

In this season, there is something else critically needed—forgiveness. Forgiveness is not about condoning poor behavior. It's about accepting our faults, embracing reality, and choosing to move past wrongs so that we are no longer victims. Brent likes to say that anyone can be victimized, but becoming a victim is a choice. Don't be a victim.

Making a choice to lay aside intense feelings of resentment is necessary to grow closer. It is a choice that benefits peace of mind.

One night Brent and I had a serious discussion. I wasn't happy, so left the dinner table and slammed the door behind me. He let me cool off a bit and came in, gently. And then I let him have it.

I had piled up his offenses from that day. I piled up his offenses from last week. And last month. Last year. Even ten years ago. He didn't stand a chance.

Never mind that I had wronged him. Never mind that we misunderstood each other's motives and actions. Never mind that my responses were loaded and undergirded by unresolved anger. I found my voice, and said what I wanted to say. He had been indicted, underwent a trial in my mind, and deserved a harsh sentence.

So, why did I feel crappy? The self-pity that motivated me felt empty. The hurt I saw on his face and the angst I heard in his voice reverberated in my mind and made my heart burn. Tears of a different kind stained my cheeks. Then in my silent prayers, I thought, "Perhaps it's time to forgive him—for what he hasn't done." And suddenly, I knew that was the problem.

Brent is a good man. He loves his kids, and he loves me. He works hard at this, and tries to do what's right, even when it isn't popular. He's provided for us, he's been loyal, hardworking, and a great husband and father. He's a successful man who is dedicated to his work. But when it comes down to his motivation, he does it all for us.

Sometimes I want the fairy tale. To be adored. Swept off my feet. To be number one. To be known to the point that he would know exactly how I feel and know exactly what to do or say to comfort/inspire me. That kind of love takes a lot of time and effort. A constant and habitual focus. Looking beyond many things that happen day to day. Kind of like when we were dating!

But in real life, this is entirely unrealistic. When it doesn't happen, I sometimes throw my pity party and complain that he doesn't do x, y and z, completely ignoring the fact that he does a, b, and c. Regularly. Faithfully. And well.

I know deep down these expectations aren't fair. I can't expect this from him or anyone else. It isn't right to judge him for the way he loves me, nor for how he doesn't. I choose to accept the love he gives, and then return it tenfold the best I know how.

Forgiving is the first step. Many times we have to forgive for something each other does that hurts. But in this case, I was angry at the absence of something, and I needed to forgive Brent for not meeting my expectations. Subtle anger had crept in and sabotaged our relationship. I was looking for something—anything to justify that anger. Once I forgave and then shut the door on those toxic thoughts, my anger subsided, the sun came out, and it was a beautiful life!

When Conflict Gets Physical (Warning: Strong Content)

Domestic violence became a topic of discussion everywhere when the video emerged of NFL player Ray Rice knocking out his fiancé in a hotel elevator. Domestic abuse is a reality that happens in the homes of approximately one in four police families.[10] I was surprised by this statistic. Most of the officers I know do not seem like they would ever engage in such behavior. But anyone can put on a good act for others.

There are a few gals I know that have varying degrees of abuse going on with their husbands. I've been surprised because there are some that I wouldn't have guessed this was the case. They're pretty good at keeping it together when others are around.

There are similarities between these men. First, they came from a father that did not treat his wife as an equal. In fact, the overall attitude was that they were of lesser value, a nuisance, or an obstacle to what he really wanted to do.

Second, there was a pornography addiction. Porn tends to portray women as servants to the almighty penis, ready to perform any way, anytime. I apologize for the crass nature of that comment, but this is true. Porn inflames an already inherent bias towards women in that it idolizes the man's conquering sexual appetite.

---

10 http://womenandpolicing.com/violencefs.asp. There are differing views on statistics of police family violence because of the discrepancies in reporting. Many cases are handled off the record or filed differently to help the officer keep his job. See also http://www.policeone.com/health-fitness/articles/1350610-Domestic-violence-in-police-families-Causes-effects-intervention-strategies/.

The third thing I have seen actually makes me ill, in that these men justify themselves with the idea that wives are subservient to their husbands, which in turn is used to justify their poor behavior. The fact that these guys are police officers—given authority to take control of situations by force when necessary—helps to twist an already twisted perspective—that a wife needs to be controlled and sometimes forced into submission.

If there is physical violence going on in your home, you already know you've got a problem. Unless you do something about it, it will continue. There are also several other forms of abuse that are subtler, and could eventually lead to violence. Here are some questions to ask yourself if you are being abused or at risk of such[11]:

- Does your partner embarrass you with put-downs?
- Are you or your children afraid of your partner?
- Does your partner control whom you talk to or where you go?
- Has your partner demanded you stop seeing family members or friends?
- Does your partner control you with money such as withholding it, taking it, or refusing to give you money?
- Does your partner make all the decisions, or do you discuss and decide together?
- Does your partner threaten you with taking away or hurting your children?
- Does your partner prevent you from working or attending other functions?
- Have you filed any charges against your partner?
- Has your partner threatened to commit suicide so that you would relent?
- Does your partner see you as his personal property?
- Did your partner witness domestic abuse in his home growing up?
- Has your partner threatened to kill you?
- Has your partner pressured you sexually for things you doesn't feel comfortable with?

11 Adapted from www.manupcrusade.com.

- Has your partner done any of this while under the influence of drugs or alcohol?

If you've answered yes to any of these questions, you may be a victim of abuse. If you turn these questions around, you may be abusing your spouse. Both men and women abuse.

On its face, domestic abuse seems to be about anger. Many times anger is what is exhibited, but it is much more than this. It's learned and modeled behavior that the abuser has been trained (intentionally and unintentionally) to treat as acceptable. It's fundamentally viewing others as having less value. It's seeing others as property rather than a partner, and even sometimes it's about reducing a person to a sexual object.

It's really about the way an abuser thinks that determines these actions. And it can be exasperated by difficulties at work, substance abuse, stress, and soul wounds.

There are many programs available for preventing and protecting domestic abuse victims. Programs and help for abusers exist as well. It will require an attitude change, professional therapy, time and patience, but this behavior can stop. I have several programs listed on my website in the resource section for both victims and abusers.

Restoration of Your Home

When your marriage has been dysfunctional for way too long, there are things that are broken that you and your spouse don't have a clue how to fix. You need a renovation of your marriage.

I like Nicole Curtis of HGTV's Rehab Addict. It's not that she's a little blonde badass who loves power tools and runs marathons. It's not that she's stubborn with her vision, or that she sports a Midwestern accent, or that she lives in Minnesota. It's that Nicole Curtis looks at old homes that others have deemed as doomed and is willing to put in the work to make them pretty again.

She braves old basements, salvages what she can, and pours new foundations. She is sure to comment that working with a shovel is a great core workout. She opens up walls to expose old brick, cleaning it up with a wire brush, and patching holes in the mortar. She designs the rooms around the brick, using it as a focal point. It's beautiful. She pulls up linoleum and exposes hardwood flooring, meticulously refinishing and repairing the old wood. The timeless beauty of the home emerges. She appreciates the splendor of old things, restoring them to let them shine in their craftsmanship, and adding both old and new to give a home the best of both.

Nicole once restored a home damaged by arson. The fire had spread to the house next door. When the damage was left unaddressed, old homes throughout the street were abandoned and boarded up.

Much like the tendency in our own homes, when the fires of conflict or neglect torch a home and the damage is done, many choose to just scrap it all and walk away. But it isn't just the couple alone that suffers. Lasting damage breeds destruction to those around them.

When there is reconciliation—when a couple decides to salvage their marriage, patiently doing the work to look at both the good and the bad in their relationship and purpose to restore it, there is something amazing that happens. There is a quality and beauty there, and a mature character that something (or someone) new just can't measure up to.

Whether we've been married three months or thirty years, our marriages could use a little tender loving care—sprucing up what's in good condition, repairing damage, and a few new changes.

Perhaps you've been broken for so long, it seems there's nothing left in your relationship. You've been unable to move past the problems, and there is bitterness and separation. One or both of you are done. Think of your marriage as an old neglected house. The tendency is to think that your house is too far-gone. It should be condemned. But if one person comes in, sees the value and is willing to do the work, your "house" could be beautiful again. It can spread to the other person in the marriage and he/she may join in. Commitment, time, patience and hard work can get it there.

If your marriage needs restoration, please read on. Perhaps you'll find yourself in between the pages of this book and find a glimmer of hope. Perhaps you can pinpoint the damage, look at what caused it, and then do a renovation with new tools, renewed attitudes, and a new, improved plan.

Brent and I know a couple that did this very thing.

The *Second* Marriage

There were problems from the start. Adam was a social worker who was laid off just a few months before his wedding to Kathy. He took the opportunity to do what he'd dreamed about as a little kid—to become a police officer.

Kathy had a very different expectation of the life she and Adam would share. She wanted to lead a quiet life with a nine-to-five job, steady income and white picket fences. A cop? Really?

To make matters worse, Adam's department had some budget issues soon after he was hired, and he was let go. Out of work for a time, Kathy tried to convince Adam to go back to social work. But he had gotten a taste of what he really loved and wasn't interested. He was a cop.

In time, he secured a position with a police department. As low man on the totem pole, he was assigned to the graveyard shift. From that time forward, Kathy developed a grudge against police work. She closed herself off to the department, his love for his career, and eventually Adam.

Seven years and two kids into their marriage, Kathy wasn't happy. They went to their pastor for counseling, but because of their tight budget, they couldn't afford what he recommended. Their pastor instead introduced them to Brent and I. We met with Adam and Kathy for about a year, mentoring them individually and as a couple. Things seemed resolved for a while.

At nine years and three kids, Adam was done. He'd grown tired of the "double life" he was expected to live—two different people at work and at home. One night, after a scuffle in a dark alley with a suspect, he showed up late at home. The way he remembers it, Kathy didn't ask about the cuts and bruises. She did ask, however, if he was given overtime for the hours away. Kathy, by the way, has no recollection of this interaction.

Sometime after that, he turned to someone who understood what he was going through—a female officer who was also experiencing marital issues. It developed into an affair. Adam spent his workout time with his new friend. This also created some workplace issues, but he didn't care. He finally felt understood.

Adam moved out. Kathy called us immediately. The four of us met together. It was awkwardly clear he was already gone. But he agreed to meet with my husband separately. I met with her as well. It was profoundly painful to witness.

They almost reluctantly agreed to try one more time. They found a great counselor with financial assistance from her parents. Kathy read my book and realized that she was actually reading about herself. He ended the affair as he realized Kathy was finally ready to accept him as a police officer. Through a slow, sometimes grueling process, both came to realize they still loved one another.

Adam moved back home. Kathy went on a ride along. She met some of his co-workers. They are now continuing to build what they call their *second* marriage, even adding one more child to their new life.

Practical Steps to Restoration

If you and your spouse are in a difficult place, there are objective things you can do to work towards making it better.

First, take inventory of what you have that is salvageable. What is good about your relationship?

Second, pinpoint the problem. This is best done together, by the way. Both of you each have your opinions as to what is wrong in your relationship. You may need to have a third party present to help you both get to the root issues.

When you're talking, determine if the issues are problems are outside factors, factors within, or both. Outside factors would be your living situation, job-related issues like schedule or hobbies that take precious time from you as a couple. If outside factors are the culprit, then you may want to do some restructuring. Is there something you need to subtract from your life together that will make a significant difference? A person or persons, a commitment that has taken priority, or perhaps children's activities? How about a TV Show or limiting time on the computer? What about adding something that will help? Like committing to meals around the table once a day (any meal)? Or adding a walk three times a week? What about date nights? Occasionally a little restructuring is all you need.

But what if the problems are inside factors? Like you're in the disillusionment stage? Or you are holding on to unrealistic expectations? Or your spouse did something that you just can't let go of? Some issues are relatively minor, and can be talked through and given a solution.

But what if it's more serious, like your partner is beating you? Or your alcohol abuse is taking its toll? An affair? Then you have a choice. Are you still committed? Enough to get help? According to marriage expert Dr. John Gottman, couples wait on average about six years too long to get help.[12] By then the animosity is so built up, the couple is ready to call it quits. Get help now—don't wait.

Wherever your marriage is at, there is information, help, and resources for police families. On my website, I've listed several seminars, books, organizations and support groups you may want to check out. Many departments have recommended therapists that understand the law enforcement life. If not, contact us via my website, and we will try to track down someone in your area.

———✛———

Discussion Questions

1. How can conflict be a way to burn or build bridges?
2. What is it that you and your spouse argue about? Is it resolved? Why or why not?
3. Is there something you need to forgive your spouse for?
4. What new ideas or aha moments are sparked by this chapter?

---

12 *Why Marriages Succeed or Fail...and How You Can Make Yours Last,* Simon & Schuster, 1994.

CHAPTER 8

It's Complicated: When Work Comes Home

It's been several years now since our incident but that doesn't mean we don't have times when he gets an edge in his voice, or his hackles stand up. Thankfully we both have come to recognize the signs and can openly dialog about it. I will run interference for the household and ask for a timeout, remind him we are on the same team, not one of the parolees or street thugs he faces daily.

LOLA, CALIFORNIA

The job takes a toll on the LEO and impacts the family in ways you'll never expect. The changes in me and the people I worked with were profound and usually forced on us so we could do the job and survive to go home at the end of our shift.

JOHN, SOUTH CAROLINA

Rick was the toughest cop in the room. He'd been on the force for a quarter of a century and had earned respect among his peers. He prided himself in the fact that he kept it together. But there was always a picture in the back of his mind of a little girl and her father that burned to death following a traffic accident while he stood by helpless to save them. The intensity of the fire prevented him from attempting a meaningful rescue. For 20 years he kept it inside—until my husband asked him the right question. As he opened up, the tears spilled and made room for relief.

He'd never even told his wife that he attended the little girl's funeral. For years it ate at him. When he was ready, he let it go in the presence of several of his fellow coworkers. It was a powerful moment for all.

There will be incidents that, for whatever reason, will insert themselves into our officers' minds and sear the images on their hearts. There will be pain, maybe even sorrow. It will depend on whether your spouse is open to admitting and talking about these things whether they fester for years as in Rick's case, or are dealt with before they bring on destructive ways of coping.

You may have heard the tongue-in-cheek phrase about motorcycle cops: "There are two kinds of motors: those who've gone down and those who *will* go down." It's like a law enforcement career in general: those who have had some kind of difficulty on the job and those who will. In a 20-30 year career, your officer *will* suffer because of this job. Injury, long-term effects of hypervigilance, bad leaders, burnout, post-traumatic stress, politics, grief over fallen comrades, and other difficulties will at some point take a toll.

As partners at home, we have to be strong. We have to keep a watchful eye out for red flags and differences in our officer's behavior. We know them, inside and out. Spouses are like compasses—we know better than anyone when our officers are going off course. But we have to pay attention. We have to know what to look for. We also must have a game plan for intervention and the courage to act.

Paying Attention

At some point, your officer will have to face something bigger than himself. He's been involved in a combat shoot. He's first on the scene of a line of duty death and had to perform CPR. He is under investigation by Internal Affairs. Or he's seen too many victims, too many stupid decisions, been in too many pursuits, or he's just sick of stupidity. In each of these situations, and many others like them, he is affected. So are we—whether he chooses to share what happened with you or not.

Carla shared her sense about a difficulty her husband was going through. "I feel Brian," she confided. "He doesn't say much, but I feel it. I can sense the stress emitting from him."

I have been there often in my years with Brent. He doesn't have to say a word and I can sense his inner turmoil about something the moment he walks in the room. I feel it—it's as real as words. If we pay attention, we can feel something is not quite right. It might be invisible to the eye, but it is very real. It's also a very good thing.

We must at least ask the question—are you upset? What happened? Best case scenario, he blurts it out. Don't panic—listen. Give a hug. Or perhaps your officer may not be quite ready to voice his pain. Perhaps he doesn't plan to. Find the balance of asking without nagging, being open for when he is ready. A calm response helps—it may be the worst news possible, but there are times to lose it and times to straighten the backbone. We match them. If he's silent and doesn't want to deal with it, we may have to learn to be patient, but be on the alert for signs of danger, ready to call for extra backup.

Knowing What to Look For

Because of the significance of our role and the intimacy with which we share, we have to know what to look for. Red flags. Symptoms. Something that will nudge our insides or be heavy on the brain. I will address the most common areas of struggle that law enforcement have tendencies toward: job stress and burnout, line of duty death and its grief, soul wounds, critical incidents, politics or office drama, injuries, and post-traumatic stress. Next chapter we'll look at suicide.

Job Stress and Burnout

We all have stress—responses to day-to-day things that life hands us that cause us to worry and hurry. There are varying levels depending on the seasons that we go through—health concerns, death of loved one, kid issues, financial pressures, and so on. Responsibilities will sometimes be overwhelming, no matter if we are in a career or raising kids at home (and many times, both).

But our officers, over years of policing, can develop what is called cumulative stress. Dr. Ellen Kirschman describes cumulative stress as "prolonged, unrelieved wear and tear that results from having more demands than a person can respond to."[13] This is common for officers—the longer they're on the job, the more they see. Typically, the officer will deal with all kinds of things for many years. The stress takes its toll in different ways, but the officer is functional. Then, something happens that tips the scales slightly, and the built up stress spills out all over the place.

Susan L. Simons of Under the Shield describes this as the Psychological Garbage Can. Every day there are things accumulated from the shift (and life in general) that get thrown in the garbage can. If the garbage can isn't emptied on a regular basis, garbage stacks up, gets stinky, and will overflow. It is cumulative stress—stress upon stress upon stress, and could break beneath its weight.

Unless your officer has a plan and a practice to relieve stress, it is coming home with him, the very second he enters the door.

For us at home it may feel like walking on eggshells. There's heaviness in the room—a cloud that hangs precariously over interactions between spouses and children. The uncomfortable mood threatens to erupt like thunder and lightening, and suddenly we know without a doubt that there is something wrong, but are afraid or unsure of how to address it for fear of the reaction.

That's not a good feeling. If this goes on for long periods of time, our relationships suffer, splinter, and work into crisis mode.

Coping with Stress

The way your officer deals with this stress makes all the difference. What are his coping mechanisms? Are those coping mechanisms healthy or unhealthy? Watch for the unhealthy. Does he stuff and stuff until it comes spewing out in elevated emotion at the worst possible time? Does he just clam up and refuse to acknowledge he's bothered? Does he douse it with a drink or three? Bury it with a large pepperoni pizza and ice cream? Distract himself with a trip to the nearest casino? Escape to that Internet site? These are examples of unhealthy coping mechanisms.

Our officers go into survival mode to deal with immediate danger, just like they were trained to do on duty. He feels uncomfortable, maybe even

---

13 Ellen Kirschman, *I Love a Cop* (New York: The Guilford Press, 2007) page 89.

pain. Coping mechanisms such as these just described give temporary respite from pain but create longer-term problems.

The first problem with unhealthy coping mechanisms is that they address symptoms, not the cause. They are a temporary fix; masks to hide pain. They are often addictive, which compounds problems.

The second problem is that these may work as survival tactics temporarily, but are detrimental to relationships at home (and his health). Isolation and moodiness often result, which cause relational distance between us. The longer these coping strategies are used, the more his perspective is warped. The more destructive coping mechanisms take it further—not only the separation because of isolation, misunderstandings and mistreatment, but actually wounding us and our kids (i.e., gambling, substance abuse, emotional abuse and physical abuse).] Don't think this will only be at home—if the compounded problems persist, it will spill over into the career. Cops who at one time were motivated to crush crime, save lives, and alleviate human suffering become the subject of criminal and internal affairs investigations for conduct that would have been unthinkable.

It doesn't have to be this way. There are healthy ways to deal with the stress and cumulative residue. There are coping mechanisms that help and heal the body and mind, and in so doing, help our relationships.

Exercise is a great start. It restores the body and the mind. Support wholeheartedly your officer's trips to the gym. Better yet, join him—deal with your stress as well as his! Work out aggression in intensified workouts. Get out and take a run, go for a hike, lift weights alongside each other. Walks and bike rides as a family incorporate time together, reducing stress and building relationships at the same time. Take a Frisbee to the park, a baseball and gloves—just get out of the house and *move*.

Time away as a couple, as a family, and alone is good for the soul. It isn't just about time off; there should be a mental separation from the career. Have you ever noticed when off duty that he's not really off? Your officer is off the clock, but not mentally. When you get away, turn off the phone, suggest he intentionally put work on a shelf for a time, and give him time to shed the residue. Time away gives respite from the stressors and can give rest and fresh perspective. Your officer may not have much availability in different seasons of his career, but make the most of what he does have. Protect his time off, and don't waste it in front of a screen.

Talking out specific issues together is also healthy. Our officers need someone who gets it, knows him, and can give perspective. The one thing about stress is that it distorts thought processes. The issue can circle the head a dozen times, gaining speed with each turnabout. But when it's talked out, he may get a perspective that isn't readily apparent. When your officer comes to you with his stress, ask questions, allowing him to break the cycle in his brain and help to pinpoint the issues. Talking it out allows him to untangle his thoughts and iron out the thought process toward a solution. It's like the Christmas lights we take out of the box every winter. They come out a jumbled mess. It takes some time to unravel, carefully and methodically. When they are finally straightened out, we replace the burnt out bulbs to get things bright again. Our thoughts are similar.

Burnout is normal, natural, and cyclical. Recognize it, plan for it, and avoid unhealthy coping mechanisms by implementing healthier choices. You and I are in a strategic position to be the influence that our officers need to make these choices. And our own stress will be dealt with as well.

The Power of a Good Marriage

Although it was a perfect day for Clarke and Tracie to chill out in the pool, Clarke felt like he would sink beneath the weight of dread. He was struggling with the stuff he'd seen on duty. He wasn't thinking he'd kill himself, but knew he was starting to head down a dark road, and he needed help. He'd inwardly argued with himself for quite awhile before he took a risk.

"This stuff is gettin' to me, Trace. I'm not okay." As soon as it left his mouth, the weight began to lift. Until she replied in shock, "Are you kidding me?!" It was not the response he was looking for.

On the outside, Clarke was supercop. On the inside, a teen's suicide triggered a breaking point. "It was one of five suicides that day, and it was my boiling point," explains Clarke. "Everything began haunting me. Everything came out—calls from the day before, the week before, the year before, ten years before. They all came back and they came back with a vengeance. Everything I thought I had dealt with, but really just disassociated from, came back."

He'd told himself to get over it, forget it. But when he couldn't, he decided he was a coward—a loser. But he did have a great relationship with his wife, and he trusted her enough to share his pain. Although initially her response was less than ideal, by the end of the day, she understood that he acted with great courage in asking for help. After doing some research together, they found the assistance he needed.

Clarke and Tracie are now hosting police suicide prevention seminars across the country. As part of his healing, Clarke made a movie called, "The Pain Behind the Badge." It speaks to officers who have suffered silently for years. When Tracie gets up to speak, she imparts these powerful words: "Why did I ever think he was okay after 22 years on the job? The Rock of Gibraltar was crumbling, and I never saw it coming. I'm lucky he's alive."

Office Politics

One of the most stressful things our officers will deal with is office politics. We say that we are the Blue Line Family. We say we have each other's backs. But my goodness, the stories I have heard from all over this country about how the brothers and sisters can treat each other—so awful!

My friend Retina says, "Yes, we are a family, but we are as dysfunctional as any other family!" Sibling rivalry, stepping on each other to get ahead, lying to cover our butts or to look better than others, grudges held for years, being patronized, and of course, favoritism are some of the causes of our internal dysfunction. The challenge—and the opportunity—in the law enforcement community is that they hire from the human race!

Brent and I have our stories—we have not been immune to politics in his 30 years. There have been many times that I have been incredibly hurt and angry with certain people for the things they've done to my husband. But my desire for retaliation doesn't help. My anger doesn't solve anything. I am powerless to affect the situation, no matter how much I want to tell somebody off, or how much in the moment I want him to be in another profession. As it is said, the grass always seems greener on the other side of the fence. Perhaps you have your own stories and hurts. Let's look at constructive ways to approach this challenge.

Six Keeps for Dealing with Politics

A keep was a type of fortified tower built within castles during the Middle Ages. This fortified residence served as a refuge of last resort should the rest of the castle come under attack.

We, too, want to have fortified residences; a refuge when our families are threatened by external adversaries. When politics affect your officer, it can dig deepest—because the hurt is personal. Your officer depends on the others in uniform he works with, and trust is essential. When another uniform breaks that trust in any way—it can feel like betrayal.

Our homes are important in this regard. When trust is broken at work, the home is a keep. There are things we can do as spouses to fortify our castle. Here are six *keeps* to help do that:

- **Keep House.** This is practical and tangible. When we understand the stressors at work, we can work to ease stress at home. We can keep a clean home—uncluttered (have a place for everything), smelling good, and orderly. I've learned over the years that Brent's stress is reduced when the toilets are clean, he has a clean shot to park, and dinner is on its way to the table. Sometimes I don't have time for anything else, so these are priorities. For those of you who work outside the home, this requires prioritization and delegation of duties to others in the home—including your officer!
- **Keep Listening.** Active listening, undistracted as possible, is an incredible gift to your spouse. Listen with the intent to understand, paying attention to body language as much as the words. Honor confidentiality.
- **Keep Anger in Check.** I once shut Brent down in the middle of his honest venting by spewing my anger towards a coworker. I had to learn to keep my feelings in check, and deal with my anger differently. It helped most when I forgave that person, something I've had to do more than once. I've heard of police wives calling up sergeants and letting them have a mindful. Please don't do that—you will do more harm than good. Brent will also remind me that there are two sides or more to every story. Just because he's frustrated doesn't mean he didn't contribute to the problem. A little humility goes a long way.

- **Keep Eyes Open.** Offer tidbits of wisdom in appropriate moments. Remind them of similar situations or facts they may have forgotten. If you have a thought of why someone acts the way they do, ask clarifying questions or say, "I wonder if..." I have sparked new thoughts and aha moments for him on several occasions—you can too.
- **Keep Confidences.** Don't share what your officer says with ANYONE that is remotely connected with the office. It will likely come back to haunt him, and you. If someone tries to bait you, smile and defer them to your officer.
- **Keep Praying.** You may not have all the information that it takes to maneuver the situation. But there is Someone who does know. God sees the past, the present, the future, and He sees the hearts of all. Pray for your husband—for his stress, for wisdom, his character, and his protection. We can also pray for ourselves—that we have mental poise—meaning self-control, grace, and wisdom in the midst of all situations. And we can pray for our families, for law enforcement leaders, and for the peace and safety of all who serve in this noble profession.

Line of Duty Death (LODD)

The following section was written by Erika Lolkus, former president of National Alliance for Law Enforcement Support. It is an incredible example of going through a LODD alongside her husband, a deputy with the Fresno County Sheriff's Department:

> *February 25.*
> *The mere mention of this date takes my breath away. It doesn't matter what year it is connected to. Since 2010 that date has been etched in my heart.*
> *February 25.*
> *Those words plague me with a myriad of emotions. Sorrow. Fear. Longing. Anger. Pride. Pride? Yeah, that's mixed in there, too.*
> *February 25, 2010.*

The day the world lost a good man. The day my husband lost another partner. The day a part of me died, too. The part of me that still believed that there is meaning in all things. That good would always triumph over evil. That my husband would always come home to me.

February 25, 2010.

It started like every other day. I kissed my husband goodbye and settled in with the kids. We quickly made it through our morning routine and were sitting down to lunch. My one-year-old in her highchair and my two-year-old teetering on a kitchen stool. My biggest worry was that his little butt would manage to slide off the stool and he'd either be hurt or spill his lunch all over the floor... or maybe both.

Just after 11 am I received a call from my husband. Not unusual, he's thoughtful and likes to check in on the kids and I. I immediately noticed the tone of his voice. Not panic. Not fear. Something more along the lines of desperation. I asked him what was wrong. My husband is a police officer. He is the calm in the storm. Desperation is not an emotion he is familiar with. If that's what I was hearing in his voice, then something was most assuredly wrong.

He said the words all police wives fear most, "There's been a shooting. It's Wally. He's dead."

Those words still haunt me. I hear them now just as clearly as I heard them then. My mind still tries to deny them just as it did on February 25, 2010. My response made no sense. I said, "Yeah, but he's going to be all right, right? He's going to be okay?" My ears couldn't properly convey those horrible words to my brain. My poor husband had to tell me again that Wally didn't make it, that the situation was ongoing, and that his instinct as a recently retired SWAT operator was to go to the scene and get the bastard that killed Wally. Instead, he was forced to do his job and stay where he belonged, consoling his team, his brothers.

I got off the phone with him knowing that he wasn't okay. Knowing that neither of us would be okay for a very long time. I turned on the news, wanting to get as much information on the situation as possible. The media soon began covering the story and I knew I had to turn off the TV. As much as I wanted to know what was going on, I knew that I couldn't expose my children to this tragedy. They were too young. They shouldn't have to worry about their daddy not making it home safely. They shouldn't have to learn that police officers get murdered. They were babies and they deserved to keep their innocence for just a little while longer.

My phone continued to ring. Every call and text seemed to bear more bad news. Another officer had been killed, this one from a neighboring town. The situation wasn't resolved for several hours. All I wanted was to have my husband home with me. I needed to hold him. I couldn't make everything better. I couldn't bring Wally back. I couldn't bring the other officer back. I felt so incredibly helpless. I knew my husband was hurting and I couldn't even be with him while he hurt.

I finally got word that the situation was over. I continued to care for my children and got them ready for bed. My husband finally walked through the door and I did all I could do—I held him and mourned with him. We got dressed, left the kids with a sitter and went to be with our blue family. I don't know that we were needed there, but we certainly needed to be there surrounded by others that were feeling all the things we felt.

I'm not sure how we made it through the rest of the week. Somehow we managed. My husband stood by Wally's parents during the most difficult days of their lives. I watched him set aside his own heartache to ensure that they had everything they needed in the weeks and months following their son's death. I know it wasn't easy for him. I know that he was under a great deal of stress. I also know that he wouldn't have had it any other way. Wally was his friend, his brother. Wally would have wanted to know that his parents were taken care of and that's what my husband was committed to doing.

In two days it will be February 25th. Seven years have gone by since Wally was killed. So much has happened since that awful day. So many other officers have been killed during these last seven years. My heart still hurts when I reflect on those days. From *a distance I've watched Wally's family learn to live without him. I've seen his beautiful wife take on a grace and dignity that is so common amongst the wives of the fallen. I've seen his brothers in blue continue to celebrate his memory in their own unique way. I'm sure Wally would approve of their new tradition. I'm equally sure that he wouldn't want us to spend February 25th mourning his death. So this year I'm going to hike up my big girl panties. I'm going to go for a run in his honor. Running was his thing and he led me to it. In the years following his death I found that the only way I could truly find peace was by running. He blessed me with this hobby so on February 25th I will run and remember him. Then I will sit and have a beer with my husband. I'll listen as he tells one of his favorite Wally stories and I will try to fight back the tears that are sure to come. Mostly, I will look for the good in the world because that is what Wally stood for and that is the best way I can think of to honor his memory.*

Wow! Let's reflect on that a bit. Erika captures so many emotional realities in this prose. Shock. Grief. Remembrance. Duty. And even hope in the honoring of heroes.

You and I understand the risks of this job. We as police families hope against hope that death doesn't come knocking on our doors, or on doors of those who are close to us.

But, for some, it does.

Grief is real, and we can't plan for it. With every somber note from the bagpiper, every missing man aircraft formation, and the echoes of a 21-gun salute, there is a pain that resonates beneath that badge. It is a reminder of the frailty of life. A reminder that the uniform is in fact, fallible. We are reminded that some good men and women will lose their lives protecting our communities.

After two Sacramento area deputy sheriffs were murdered in October 2014, many officers struggled to cope with this loss. Some shut down. Some visited the gravesite and sat for hours, trying to make sense of it. For those who may have been on scene, the image of a fallen brother leaves a deep pain.

For the families, it was tough as well. There were critical incident debriefs, some for officers, and some for extended families. It was heart wrenching to hear what some of these officers saw and felt, and to hear how spouses and moms and dads felt when they heard the news. A couple of wives decided to open a home to other wives from the department—to just sit, have a cup of coffee, and talk. Ninety women showed up, and soon a wives group developed for their department. Two years after the fact, they invited me to speak about how to support our officers in critical incidents. There were a couple gals who were close to the fallen who could struggled not to leave, as the pain and fallout was still so fresh.

In the heartbreak of that incident, and so many others like it that have happened along our officer's career, we must make room for the toll of grief and pain. But we don't have to do it alone...we weren't meant to.

Grieving Alongside Others

The thunder rumbled and the room lit up. She sighed heavily, leaning over to see that her husband was not in bed. And then she remembered where he was. Sadness. Anger. Grief.

She pulled herself from under the covers. She couldn't sleep anyway. Between the physical storm that presently ripped through the sky, and the storm that had crashed in on their world just a few hours earlier, there was no peace in slumber. There was no peace anywhere. She and her husband were reeling from the loss of a Blue Line brother, and extended family member.

The days that followed were confusing, her husband dealing with not only a personal loss but also a professional one. Emotions alternated between shock, anger, and sadness. They went through the motions with arrangements, and protocol, and the overwhelming presence of uniforms, all with their confused children in tow. It was devastating.

"I don't know what to do," confided Kristin about her husband. "He's all business. He's short with the kids. I know he's hurting, but he won't allow himself to grieve."

This is very common for peace officers. Some will allow themselves to grieve, some won't. Your officer may need permission to grieve. He may push it off, and then grieve later. Here are a few ideas to help those who grieve:

- **Be available.** Let him tell stories. Let him say he misses the fallen. Allow him to be angry at injustice. Sharing these feelings does two things: It takes away the power to rule his thoughts, and it brings him closer to you. Grief is something to be shared.
- **Attend Police Week in Washington DC.** Every May thousands of police officers and survivors of the previous year's fallen head for the capitol to honor the sacrifice they gave. There are events all week long to take part in. Attend the vigil and memorial service. Ride a bike in memory of the fallen, or run the 5K. Get a name etching from the Law Enforcement Memorial Wall. Leave a note or memento by the name of whom you grieve. Sit at the wall awhile. It's worth the time and money. Sharing this experience will bring you together in a different way than before.
- **Expect unexpected emotion**. As time passes, shared grief will subside. Sometimes feelings of loss will rise up here and there even years later. This is normal.
- **A few additional pointers to help those who are grieving:**
  - Being present means everything.
  - They don't need to hear the upside view of things. At this moment there is no bright perspective—their lives have been forever changed.
  - They don't need someone to force them to eat. The body shuts down the need for food in the initial stages of shock and grief. They will eat eventually. Hand them a bottle of cold water instead.
  - They don't need advice. Solutions will present themselves soon enough. Let grief have its moments.
  - Don't pass judgment on how they grieve. Every person grieves differently.
  - Allow them to talk without interruption, cry as softly or loudly as need be, be silent and quiet as thoughts untangle. Offer a comforting touch or hug if appropriate. Sometimes the best way to comfort your husband is to have sex.

- Share short positive memories or compliments of the person lost when appropriate.
- Share photos of the deceased.
- After the memorial services have passed and the world moves on, it's important that they are not forgotten. Cards are best sent a month or two after the death. Flowers at Christmas in memory of the person lost, a tribute of some kind, or a phone call—it's never too late to reach out to those who've lost someone significant.
- In recent years, officers have shown up in uniform to support the children of the fallen at daddy-daughter dances, graduations, career day at school—standing in for the deceased. Your wholehearted support will be appreciated. What a beautiful way to remember the fallen.

Grief, in all its anguish, is a normal, natural part of life. It is not something to avoid, but to make time to embrace and work through unhurried. When there is loss in your blue or blood family, whether your officer or you, or both, join hands and walk together.

Critical Incidents & Trauma

A critical incident is a specific event that overwhelms an officer's ability to cope effectively. Examples include accidents that have multiple fatalities or that involve children, a mass casualty incident (like 9/11), an officer-involved shooting, death of a co-worker, or in Rick's case, a little girl in a car that was engulfed in flames. Critical incidents happen frequently in police work. In response, many departments have seen the value of implementing Critical Incident Stress Debriefings (CISDs). This is done shortly after the incident occurs, usually within a few days. Officers gather with a therapist or certified individual to talk about what happened, and how it is affecting each person.

CISDs help in several ways. First, they acknowledge the significance of the incident. Second, they unmask the "fog of war"—officers will perceive things that may or may not be reality during the incident. Sometimes these perceptions develop deep feelings of guilt or shame. When the truth is shared, those feelings subside. Third, they open up conversation about how the incident affects officers emotionally. This is so good. For most of our law enforcement history, the emotional effects of trauma have been labeled as weakness, or worse. But officers are not robots; they are human beings with multiple aspects—physical, emotional, mental, and spiritual. It is a good thing to acknowledge this and act accordingly.

For some, participating in a CISD is all that is needed. But for many others, the trauma of an incident may cause psychological and emotional injury that requires additional help.

Steve was involved in an incident that included a fireman who wanted to commit suicide-by-cop. It included a highly charged pursuit and violent gunfight that ended when Steve shot and killed the man. It was someone he'd worked with before. That night changed his life—and not for the better. His family fell apart and friends fell away when he isolated himself. He had a couple affairs. He felt a need to make it right with the other firemen. Confusion, anger, and grief were new companions. He had sight and smell triggers. He had no tolerance for light-hearted play with guns. He had to deal with grand juries and trials. It all adds up to a long recovery from one fateful incident.

Steve's suicide-by-cop incident encompasses many of the symptoms and fallout of a critical incident. But Steve recovered. He is still working, has promoted a couple of times, and has built a successful career, even making changes in his department for better responses to future critical incidents.

His department provided a CISD, but failed to follow up in their communication thereafter. Steve feels it's important to keep in contact during leave otherwise abandonment and punishment are negative adds to the list of already difficult circumstances.

Steve had a support system in place that was the most valuable resource he found during the fallout. He attempted counseling, which is recommended.

A key component with Steve's long-term healing was that he moved on in his journey through helping others. When a person who has been through something huge can move on to help or serve others with similar experiences, deeper healing occurs. This requires vulnerability and courage to defy the enemy of isolation. The natural tendency is to pull away, feeling misunderstood and alone. Connection with those who've been there is crucial to moving forward.

Responses to Trauma

Responses to trauma come in many forms. If your officer has been through a critical incident, or a string of seemingly small but bothersome incidents, or memories plague him from years ago, understand that any of these symptoms he may be experiencing are normal reactions to something abnormal.

Law enforcement culture is changing to understand and help those who've experienced trauma. Peace officers want to help people, and sometimes that just isn't possible. People die. Crime is destructive. Tragedies happen. It's part of the job, and they feel the effects. That doesn't make them weak; it confirms they're human.

Dr. Todd Langus, a retired police officer turned therapist explains it like this, "After trauma, we cops have a realization that we are vulnerable. There is helplessness, which equals a loss of control, which translates to 'I failed.' We're trained that way. And we care. Any cop worth his salt will end up in my office after trauma."

As spouses, we are the backup at home. We are the first responders to the scene when the job has become overwhelming in this regard. When trauma happens, things are unsettled. Life is disrupted. And you will probably bear some of the brunt of this. It's the risk we take as cop wives. But we are not alone. Read on, there is hope!

Post-Traumatic Stress (Disorder)

Post-Traumatic Stress (PTS) is a condition that results from a critical incident or develops as a result of repeated exposure to trauma. In his book *CopShock, Second Edition: Surviving Post-traumatic Stress Disorder* Allen Kates says that "one in three cops may suffer from PTSD, a condition that could lead to depression, suicidal thoughts, addictions, eating disorders as well as job and family conflict."[14] Some of the common symp-

---

14 http://www.copshock.com/description.php

toms include anger, nightmares, flashbacks, concentration problems, emotional detachment, and avoidance of people and places.

Reactions to trauma are normal, but if they persist over three months, become disruptive in your officer's life, or cause him extreme distress, then he may be experiencing the effects of Post-Traumatic Stress Disorder (PTSD). The difference between PTS and PTSD relates to severity and duration.

For those of us who are not in the mental health field, we can be guilty of transposing PTS and PTSD. They are very similar, after all. In fact, there is confusion because there are several different labels for duty-induced stress, residue, and trauma—and to our untrained eyes, they all kind of look the same.

Cumulative stress (see previous section) is related to the hypervigilance rollercoaster—close brothers. If the rollercoaster is not addressed with exercise and a steady diet of balanced roles, that stress will compound for years, possibly opening the door to health problems and of course, relational issues. Cumulative stress can compound over the years—residue upon residue until a relatively insignificant incident happens, and snap—post-traumatic stress.

PTSD is diagnosed by the American Psychological Association and is considered a mental health disorder. However, I have come across many mental health professionals that do not consider it an actual disorder. As research continues into the brain and how it functions and results of therapies are considered, more and more people are looking at post-traumatic stress as an injury that can be healed. The symptoms are the body's natural and normal reaction to an unnatural or abnormal event.

The best book I've read on duty-induced PTS(D) is *The Rite of Return* by Karen Lansing, LMFT, BCETS. She explains what happens in the brain and the physiological responses to trauma, as well as recommended treatment for police officers in particular. If you suspect that your officer is experiencing PTS(D), this book is a must-read.

If our officers have PTS(D), we have no choice but to pay attention—it is life altering. But we must learn to recognize what PTS(D) looks like. There are four types of symptoms that tend to be cyclical in nature:

1) Re-experiencing: This includes nightmares and flashbacks that cause you distress. It also includes triggers—something that you hear, see or smell that takes your mind right back to the trauma.
2) Hyperarousal: This is a result of a chronic state of re-experiencing the trauma—the body is in a constant state of hyperarousal. Symptoms include insomnia, anger, exaggerated startle response, problems concentrating, and hypervigilance. The body is in survival mode, taking on the fight/flight/freeze response when threatened.
3) Avoidance: This is the behavioral response to triggers to avoid the pain and unpleasant feelings these triggers summon. This looks like avoiding crowded places and loud sounds, or depending on alcohol, drugs or other unhealthy coping mechanisms.
4) Emotional numbing: Trauma can trudge up deep emotions that are very uncomfortable. Some will experience a numbing of sorts so to adapt to these intense feelings. For some it's fear; others it's a feeling of failure or guilt.[15] This area is most difficult on relationships with others. Debby, whose husband suffers from PTSD, calls this "Poop Lasagna." His PTSD came from several incidents over his career. He experienced layer upon layer of unprocessed strong emotions that eventually resulted in emotional numbing.

John Caprarelli, a retired LAPD officer who was given the Medal of Valor for his response during the infamous North Hollywood shootout in February 1997, describes the emotional toll on him and others in the months and years following the incident:

"The muzzle of his rifle is now squarely on me. Another second, maybe a half, and it will be all over...I glance at my weapon in confused amazement. I feel like I haven't drawn a breath in minutes. My head is spinning, my chest constricted, and I can hear the blood roaring through my ears...I give it one last chance and pull back on the trigger with all that I have...Nothing.

---

15 http://www.ptsd.va.gov/public/PTSD-overview/basics/symptoms_of_ptsd.asp

"Looking at his eyes, I can see under his sweat-sodden ski mask that the corners of his eyes are crinkled. He is smiling at me! With his leather-gloved finger curled around the AK-47's trigger, it seems as though his jaw is mouthing something from behind the mask...Panic courses through me and everything goes black as the world seems instantly yanked from me...Is this it?

"Drawing one long rasp of fresh air, I feel like I have just popped to the surface after too deep of a dive in some murky waters. It is dark, I am covered in sweat, and my heart is pounding like a jackhammer...Where am I?

"My wife touches my shoulder as she asks, 'You okay?'

"'Yeah, just another dream,' I reply. 'I'm fine.'

"We both know that is not true. There is an increasing menace, one we would not understand much about or know how to handle until it had already run its course."[16]

If your officer is exhibiting any of these symptoms, acknowledge he may have PTS(D). Grasp onto the idea that yes, something isn't right, and it needs to be dealt with. Ignore the ignorant judgments of those who've either not been there, or deny it themselves. He has an injury to the brain, and like a broken arm, it needs to be reset, given time to heal, and then therapy.

Treating PTS(D)

There are several schools of thought as to how to treat those with PTS(D). As mentioned above, there are different thoughts on the word, "disorder." It is said that if we label it with the word disorder that it would bring shame to those who have it. There is a stigma with the word—it is a mental disorder, and therefore you're crazy, unstable, and unreliable. There is the fear that once an officer has the diagnosis, that his job is in danger. And in many departments, this is a justified fear.

But this isn't the case. Our bodies and brains have different ways of dealing with injuries. Some injuries need more intervention than

---

16 John Caprarelli, *Uniform Decisions*, pp. 15-16

others—and thus it is with PTS(D). It can be cured, but not if it isn't acknowledged.

"People believe that if you have PTSD that you have it forever and you cannot get better," says Becky Parkey, a counselor who works with veterans at the VA, and a cop wife. "Police departments believe this. That is not true. You *can* get better, you *can* cope with it, and things *will* get better if you have the proper treatment. However, it will get worse without the proper treatment, especially if you stuff it inside and keep living and doing what you are doing. You will suffer, your family will suffer, but if you do the work, everything will get better."

Dr. Langus highly recommends you see a counselor for PTS(D) and trauma-related issues that knows law enforcement, studies law enforcement, understands law enforcement, and has done research with law enforcement. Therapists that don't have the understanding of the tactical side of policing can miss places where the officer has been traumatized. Say he was in a combat situation but didn't shoot—a regular therapist would not know to explore the guilt/shame/fear that comes with the law enforcement mindset in that situation.

Many have achieved great success in treating PTS(D) with Eye Movement Desensitization and Reprocessing (EMDR) therapy. The EMDR Institute, Inc. describes this therapy as "a psychotherapy that enables people to heal from the symptoms and emotional distress that are the result of disturbing life experiences. Repeated studies show that by using EMDR people can experience the benefits of psychotherapy that once took years to make a difference. It is widely assumed that severe emotional pain requires a long time to heal. EMDR therapy shows that the mind can in fact heal from psychological trauma much as the body recovers from physical trauma. When you cut your hand, your body works to close the wound. If a foreign object or repeated injury irritates the wound, it festers and causes pain. Once the block is removed, healing resumes. EMDR therapy demonstrates that a similar sequence of events occurs with mental processes. The brain's information processing system naturally moves toward mental health. If the system is blocked or imbalanced by the impact of a disturbing event, the emotional wound festers and can cause intense suffering. Once the block is removed, healing resumes. Using the detailed protocols and procedures learned in

EMDR training sessions, clinicians help clients activate their natural healing processes."[17]

I mentioned Karen Lansing earlier in this chapter. In her work with law enforcement officers in Ireland, Kosovo, and the United States, she has developed a program that has produced remarkable results. She combines brain scanning, EMDR and talk therapy, and simulation training to not only cure duty-induced PTSD, but to actually return officers to duty mentally stronger and more capable to withstand critical incidents. She describes EMDR Therapy as REM sleep simulation—to simulate REM sleep in the brain, removing that blockage to promote the brain's natural tendency to heal.

Our son was diagnosed with PTSD after witnessing a horrific event in Marine Corps boot camp. Our family went to a church service on Christmas Eve, having been given tickets right next to the stage. It was loud, unpredictable, beautiful, and almost everyone loved it. Almost. Afterwards our son stormed outside and when challenged, grew irate. It was very uncomfortable. In the silence on the way home, it occurred to me what was going on. I gently asked some questions, and then realized the outburst was a response to a PTSD trigger. At that point, our son had an aha moment. He realized what was going on, apologized, and we resolved to sit in a place where a quick exit was possible, as well as distance from loud noises and surprising action. The following year we put these in place, and our son was fine.

As spouses and families, PTS(D) is a very intrusive and unwelcome houseguest. It can wreak all kinds of havoc, so the longer it reigns unfettered, the more serious the consequences. Lansing feels strongly that many marital problems that accompany or are caused by the behavior PTS(D) creates will disappear when it is fixed. Many couples will seek marital counseling before therapy for PTS(D) because it is "safer" than addressing an issue that could have career consequences. But eventually the root cause needs to be dealt with—the elephant in the room. When the officer is drinking heavily to cope with the injury to his brain, or prone to explosive anger, or blaming others for not helping his symptoms, that

---

17 https://www.emdr.com/general-information/what-is-emdr/what-is-emdr.html

will continue until the injury is fixed. For your sake and the sake of your children, get help for PTS(D), and the sooner the better.

How to Deal with His Crisis

Whatever crises our husbands undergo, they need us, and they need us to be strong. Depending on the circumstances, we could be the ones who are there for them to talk out some of the emotion. But when it's too big for us, we can come alongside and love them enough to get them the help they need. Whatever they are dealing with, they need to know they aren't alone.

Our husbands, however, may not want to be "fixed." It's their deal, and they want to work it out. In this situation, perhaps they don't understand the effects on us and our children. Maybe pride is a factor. Maybe they have adopted a cultural view that police officers are supposed to be tough and not show weakness. Sometimes they need space to work out the answer rather than depending on us too much.

Depending on your husband's department, there may be a stigma against bringing up stress. In some cases, doing so may jeopardize their career. For many years, the culture of law enforcement has been to ignore responses to trauma. These responses have been labeled as weakness. Fortunately, the thinking within law enforcement circles is gradually changing into thinking that trauma is a natural response to the unnatural incidents that our cops experience. While this new way of thinking is slowly making its way throughout the country, it isn't yet universal. If this is the case for your husband, he'll need a safe listener, and it may need to be you.

Here are practical ways you can help in the aftermath of trauma:

Right after the trauma:

- **Be quiet.** Your officer is on overload and can't handle conversation. It won't be like this forever. Sitting quietly, laying beside them, softly touching him if he's okay with that, all are considered a ministry of presence. This is comforting.

- **Listen.** When he is ready to talk, be available. Your time and attention are a much-needed gift. Liz's husband Scott had been through a horrible trauma on duty. Her immediate thoughts were, "It's not about me; it's about him. My job right now is to match him. If he needs to cry, let him cry. If he's angry, let him be angry." This loans our officers our strength and inner fortitude. It gives them a safe place—a foundation from which they will need to get up off the pavement and begin to walk again. As an aside, Liz didn't cry for two and a half days—her emotions were put on hold in survival mode while she was there for her husband. The tears came later. This is absolutely normal!
- **Ensure he sleeps.** Sleep is the body and brain's natural healing process. Do whatever you have to do to get him some sleep. Alcohol seems like it will help, but it doesn't. Alcohol will make him tired, but inhibits REM sleep, which is exactly what is needed for the brain to heal.
- **Ask for help from others.** Meal trains. Child care. Family pitching in. You can't do this alone.
- **Create that safety zone**. Liz and Scott were given a hotel room for a weekend to hide away for a couple days to gain their bearings. Liz asked if they could have a hot tub in the hotel room as she thought this would help him relax. That's exactly what it did.
- **Have sex.** There's something about trauma that brings about the need for survival sex. Oblige him—he needs it more often with a deeper intensity. As spouses, we are the only ones who can comfort him in this way.

After some time:

- **Be patient.** Wait for the healing to trickle in. Pray. Some things can't be solved right away. Put aside expectations and frustration.
- **Make an appointment for him to get a physical.** Stress can take a toll on his body. Nip health problems in the bud.
- **Create delicious, healthy meals for your family.** Stress tends to increase a desire for junk.
- **Discourage making important decisions** when he is overwhelmed.

- **Maintain normalcy with life.** Routine can keep balance in the midst of trials.
- **Get him out and about.** It may be a kayak ride on the local pond. It may be a walk in your neighborhood. A fishing trip. Camping. Something to get him out without a lot of crowds and interaction. Then eventually as he feels comfortable add places that have more people and close friends. Don't allow him to isolate. Nudge, but don't push.
- **Invest in your relationship.** Even after things subside a bit, you need to make time for the two of you and with the kids. Strength comes in togetherness, not isolation.
- **Communicate directly.** If symptoms are persisting or if he's resorting to alcohol, porn, food, prescription or illegal drug use, you must address it quickly. Find healthier solutions for prolonged symptoms.
- **Extend gracious understanding and forgiveness.** This breaks up confrontations and sometimes-uncontrolled responses.
- **Support in a way that is not codependent.** We want to understand and support them as our husbands, but that doesn't mean making excuses for their behavior. If there is a problem, treat it as reality and work toward a solution. If it's an issue like burnout he's dealing with, that could be easily identified and worked through without professionals. But if it's bigger and deeper, seek help.
- **Take advantage of programs and assistance.** Check out my website resource page for critical incident and trauma assistance on a national level. Check if your department has an employee assistance program. They are designed to help police officers get the help they need, sometimes even paying for counseling. Inquire if your husband's department has a peer support program where other officers have gone through something similar. Some departments also offer support groups for related issues. If you can't find anything in your area and are reluctant to contact the department, contact me via my website and I'll find something for you.
- **Write down your feelings through the journey.** When you're on the other side, you can look back and see how far you both have come.

As backup, we must also practice safety precautions while coming to the aid of him when he is in danger. Like supporting a loved one through surgery and recovery, so it goes for those of us who live with those who suffer from trauma.

Take Time to Recover

As you move forward after trauma, try to get some time off and get away for a change of scenery. Build positive memories. Take a break from extra-curricular activities that create more busyness. Make sure your family gets rest. If your relationship is at a relational deficit, then start making deposits.

This is also a good time to set some new boundaries relating to the issue. Perhaps you both need to stop spending time with friends who drink heavily and find other avenues for friendship. Maybe you both need to set some boundaries with activities that aggravate issues. Follow the avenues of healthy support. You also have the unique position to help him get the nourishment he needs through healthy meals and exercise. In fact, eating right and exercising are essential for his (and your) healing.

What I'm suggesting here is for the both of you. His crisis affects you in a huge way. Things you go through affect him as well because your lives are intertwined. You both need time to recover and to heal. In some cases it could be a lengthy road. You'll need this time to remain patient while the problems are resolved.

Items You'll Need in a Crisis

If you are suddenly needed at the hospital for any reason, take a moment to make sure you (and those with you) have the following:

- Cell phone and charger
- Bottle of water
- Any medications you'll need for the next 24 hours
- Purse/wallet
- A light jacket or sweater
- Toothbrush and toothpaste

- Comfortable and appropriate clothes and shoes. Don't forget to put on a bra! (Many people will be at the hospital.)
- Small toys, crayons and color books, and snacks for children
- Diaper bag and formula for infants

Unhealthy Coping Mechanisms

Through all of the stress and trauma-related problems, there will be a tendency for your officer and you to self-medicate in some way. These ways of coping can take different forms such as substance abuse, sexual addiction (porn, affairs), gambling, and overeating.

Consistently relying on drinking, drugs, sex, food, gambling, or porn as coping mechanisms, they become habits, which can soon become additions. The most important point to make here is that addictions are destructive behaviors that will have their consequences. They affect relationships, especially with those close to you. Addictions can cause financial instability, loss of trust and respect, undependability, and clouded thought processes that lead to arguments, destructive behavior, and wrong choices. All of these problems can ruin a marriage and destroy your children.

Life is hard, and it is tempting to use something to lean on, to try to get some sleep, or to mask pain. We have to keep a watchful eye on our officers, and yes, ourselves as well. The stressors on the Thin Blue Line are heavier than ever—for officers, and for us at home.

Here are symptoms of an addiction. You can ask the questions for alcohol, drug use, pornography, food, or gambling:

- How important is this activity/substance to me? Can I go without it often without thinking about it or craving it? Is it a priority in my life?
- Do I feel better or more in control when I am consuming this substance or doing this activity?
- Do I feel that I need more? Have I found that the time I devote to it is never enough?
- Could I stop without an emotional attachment to it? Does thinking about not doing it ever again make me anxious?

- Has this activity/substance disrupted my life in some way? Has a loved one complained about it? Has it affected work or relationships?
- Have I tried to quit, only to revert back to it?

These are good questions to keep you on alert to the possibility of addiction. If you find that you're answering yes to these questions, then what?

- Acknowledge you have a problem that needs a solution.
- Decide that you will stop no matter how difficult. Commit to the process of scrubbing this addition from your life.
- Understand you can't do it alone. You need accountability, comfort, and encouragement. Choose accountability partners wisely.
- Get rid of everything that is associated with your addiction. This may include some habits, places, and relationships that harbor/ encourage this behavior.
- Recognize triggers and either avoid them or develop a plan to respond to them.
- Join a 12-step program. This program is helpful to reach the root cause(s) for the addiction, and then directs action that will deal with the cause.
- Consider professional therapy, including inpatient, if the addiction seems out of control.

If you suspect that your spouse has a problem, talk with him about it when he isn't engaging in that activity. Be ready with specific examples of behavior, not generalized accusations. If he denies it, get others involved who love your husband. Have your resources lined up—phone numbers, locations of meetings and support groups, and people to contact. You can check our website for resources specifically tailored for these addictions.

Being Strong When We Feel Weak

This chapter has been pretty difficult to write, so I imagine it is also difficult to read. If you are new to the LEOW life, please don't think that you will experience every single one of these problems. There are times when this life is difficult, but there are many awesome things about sharing life together that make life so sweet. But of course, we have to be strong in those times when it's not so great.

Years ago the mentor I met with while a newlywed was diagnosed with an aggressive brain tumor. Debbie was given six months to live but died in five. During that time I too was dealing with internal hurts that needed healing. It was really tough. A wise friend of mine encouraged me to watch for what I could learn during this time. "Find purpose in the pain," she said. I'd never done that before, and in the midst of it all, it seemed impossible.

But it wasn't. With Brent's help and support, eventually I viewed the end of Debbie's life as a new beginning for me. Debbie had planted a bit of her heart into mine, and this I could hold on to. Incredibly, the final piece of my healing was put into place through a conversation at her funeral. And although I miss her even now, in a way I keep Debbie alive as I carry forward what she taught me.

When you are going through painful seasons of life, challenge yourself. Try to find purpose amidst the pain. What can you learn? What can you carry forward? How can you have victory over what seems like defeat?

When life is topsy-turvy, we need to be held up by our foundations and support system. There may be a tendency to withdraw when things are tough, but it is when we need others all the more. A timely phone call or a meal provided is very uplifting. You never know what kindnesses others will offer when you are in crisis.

As a person of faith, I turn to God for comfort. He has been my refuge and strength in the midst of some very hard times.

Kristin gave me the detailed report of how her husband's department was internally corrupt. Her husband was suffering. He'd tried to deal with it. He'd tried to make a difference. In fact, at that point he had tried just about everything, and was in misery. It was difficult walking through it all with her husband. She was in tears as she asked, "What do we do?" I gave a few suggestions, but those too were already tried. Finally, I sighed. "Kristen, sometimes you just have to walk through it one step at a time. You can't do anything but get up each morning and go to bed each night, and let it hurt. It is at those times that we just have to trust God for the future, and walk through that valley." We were both in tears, but it was actually comforted tears. At those times in life, our character grows deep. It's those times that we find peace and purpose in the pain.

The last bit of help may just come from your own attitude. It may sound strange, but when you are going through tough times, be thankful. Sometimes you might have to start with being thankful your situation isn't worse than it is! It may seem like your life is in shambles, but there is always something small (or large) to be thankful for.

Sandcastles

Whether the issues that you face in your marriage are a result of his job or relational differences or other outside pressures, there is a likelihood that at some point you will want to give up. Even the best marriages have occasional long winter seasons, and we are human.

For sixteen months, Brent lived out of town during the week while he commanded another area. Our kids were heading into their teens, and it was a lot for me to balance while he was gone. Then he transferred to a local position but took on the most challenging job of his life. I saw him more, but for the first few months he came home and promptly fell asleep on the couch. His job took more and more of his energy, concentration, and time. Then personal hard times hit. It was very difficult.

After many months of seemingly impossible demands at work and at home, I saw a change in his behavior. He became withdrawn, angry, forgetful, and, at times, almost victim-like. This wasn't like him. For a while I was concerned about him. But then I became more concerned about me.

"How long will this last?" led to "I don't want to be treated like this," which led to "I don't deserve this." That led to "I don't have to take this anymore!"

I started detaching myself, entertaining thoughts of escape. It became a big temptation that consumed several days a week. I stopped fighting for us in my mind. I was letting go, giving up. With each squabble and each letdown, I found myself drifting farther and farther away and hurting more and more.

It was the first time in our marriage that I considered leaving. It was a very strong temptation. Frankly I just wanted out. I needed relief.

We went on vacation to the beach in southern California, and I wondered how to tell him where I was. We bumped along through the week, and I felt so distant. He was in the same room, but I felt we'd grown miles apart. One day we took a trip to the zoo with the kids. As we got into the car, we had an argument, and that was the final straw. All the way home it was over for me. I'd had enough. I didn't want this anymore.

After dinner I went for a walk on the beach to clear my head. As I walked toward the ocean, I noticed a really cool sandcastle that someone had built that day. It was fortified with thick little towers around it and stones and a moat. Someone spent a lot of time building it.

The tide was coming in. A wave lapped at the fortress that surrounded it, and suddenly I was riveted. For the next hour, I watched as wave after wave washed bits of the castle away. The fortress was the first to go. Then the waves methodically carved a hole in the back of the castle I couldn't see. Suddenly the top fell off, and the waves washed it away within minutes. Then a large wave swept up, and the rest of the castle split in half. My chest tightened, and I caught a sob. My eyes filled with tears as I realized that, to me, it was not a sandcastle disappearing, but my own home.

I heard a whisper: "Are you gonna do this to your family?"

I wept as the tide completely wiped the sandcastle away, leaving only the stones that garnished the fortress. It was as if it had never existed. And I heard that still, small, but firm voice ask me again, "Are you going to do this to Brent? To your kids? Everything you've built will be for nothing. And for what?"

I looked up at the blurred stars through my tear-filled eyes. "No," I decided, "No, I cannot do this. No! I will not leave."

I listened to the waves crashing on the shore and gained a little strength.

"No, I will not do this to my husband. I will not destroy my family."

The hurt still burned in my heart. But I decided to stay. And then I decided to recommit myself to loving my husband no matter what he was going through.

After that night I had to re-train my mind to think positively about Brent and our relationship. It took a couple weeks, but then I realized that he was hurting too. He was burnt out. He was empty, weary, and he needed me! So I reached out with a new attitude and started actively loving him again even though not much changed on his end at first. I loved him first out of compassion but then with fervency.

Then things began to change. He relaxed. Work seemed to ease up. We started laughing together. Twenty days after the sandcastle moment, he presented me with a beautiful little song that he had heard and thought it could be ours. This meant so much to me! It seemed that once I decided to stay, my recommitment encouraged him and lifted him out of the place he was in.

That was many years ago. Many blessings ago. Many memories ago. Many kisses and hugs and quiet moments ago. Many smiles and fights and jokes and joys ago. It makes me so happy now to know I didn't miss all of it. I made the right choice.

Think We, Not Me

As I look back, I realize that I let myself get really self-focused. It became more about me than we. And when times are tough, this is a recipe for failure.

That night on the beach reminded me of something else. After the sandcastle disappeared, I looked to my right and saw some large rocks that some condominiums were built upon. I realized that Brent and I had built our relationship on a strong foundation of trust, mutual respect, and unconditional love. We were undergoing some strong storms of life and had been pelted and worn down. But because our foundation was strong, we would not fail. Our life together would not disappear like a castle built on sand; it would stand the test of time.

—∞∞∞—

Discussion Group Questions

1. Describe a time in which your husband struggled with his job. How did you deal with it?
2. Talk about ways you have come up with to ease his stress.
3. Next week bring copies of your favorite healthy recipe.
4. Share something you learned from a difficult time in your life.

CHAPTER 9

SUICIDE: LET'S PREVENT DISASTER

*It seemed that a pattern was evolving with officers
I had worked with in the past taking their own lives,
guys who had also been at the shootout. Three whom
I had worked the confines of a patrol car with, whom
I had joked with in the locker room and hallways
during different periods of time, had decided that
life was just too tough. These were guys who usually
had smiles on their faces. I couldn't understand it,
and though I had heard others, including the Chief,
say that the shootout had nothing to do with it, I had
my doubts. With my own baggage from the shootout
as a backdrop, I easily saw how it could have played
some part in the big picture. For someone to resort
to suicide it would require a lot of pressure and stress,
two things the shootout was generous in providing.*

JOHN CAPRARELLI, *UNIFORM DECISIONS*

*I don't know who I am anymore. It seems
I have lost something of myself.*

REAGAN, AN OFFICER WHO COMMITTED
SUICIDE THREE MONTHS LATER [18]

---

18 Excerpt from *My Life for Your Life*, Clarke A. Paris, p. 76

everal years ago, Brent and I were getting ready for bed at the end of the day when he checked his phone one last time. Another suicide. It was number fifteen for our department in a period of four years. The frequency seemed to be escalating. I cried out, "Another one?! What are we *doing*?!" I didn't know it at the time, but it was quite a prophetic question. I was referring to the department—how will *they* respond? But actually the more I thought about the question, I realized that *I* might be able to do something.

I don't know what it was about the fifteenth officer, but it seemed like everyone jumped into action. Number fifteen pushed the panic button, and we awoke. The department began talking about suicide openly. Our officers' association published a double-page ad in their monthly newsletter: "Call for Backup," with a picture of a glass of alcohol and a gun. We implemented awareness seminars across the state and set up debriefing sessions with those who knew the suicide victims. We educated ourselves. We decided as a department to hit suicide head on, deal with it as the reality it was, not a deniable secret hovering in the shadows.

In my own research, I learned that almost always the one who commits suicide just lost a significant relationship. When a life is going sideways, others are affected in a big way. Helplessness, blame, an inability to get a handle on problems, and depression (among other things) will push away those who are close. When things are falling apart, and hope seems to have gone, the natural tendency is to get out. The boat is sinking, and our survival instincts say, "Abandon ship!" Many times this is one more reason to pull the trigger.

This book is part of my own action against suicide. I care about the mental and emotional health of my husband and those on the Thin Blue Line. If by sharing my own struggles I can encourage other wives to hang tough through the hard stuff, maybe suicide won't be such an attractive option to their officers. If educating law enforcement spouses about these realities equips them to deal positively with the negatives, then perhaps marriages will be saved. If our officers know they have backup at home, perhaps they will be more courageous to get the help they need.

What to Look For

So how can we discern if our spouse is contemplating suicide? By watching and listening for the symptoms. Sometimes there are signs of PTS(D), whether from one specific incident, or a collection of events over time. If they don't deal with the trauma, they risk depression, which can be a precursor to suicide. If your officer is having trouble reconciling these thoughts, he may be at risk. According to several articles on police suicide, a typical profile of a suicide candidate is a white male (though not always), 35 years of age, separated or divorced, using alcohol or drugs, and has recently experienced a loss or disappointment. They may have made out a recent will, bought a weapon, or appear to be getting their affairs in order. There is generally a significant mood change—either better or worse. They may exhibit signs of anxiety, frustration, or confusion.

Bob, a retired fireman, recounted the days leading up to his suicide attempt. Depression and suicidal thoughts had been a constant but unwanted companion, and an addition to alcohol fueled his desire to end his life. His wife and children had left years earlier. He was alone.

He had it all planned out. He would use the very gun that his father had used many years earlier upon learning he had terminal cancer. The weapon had done the trick; it would do so again. He went out behind the garage, bringing with him a lawn chair and a beer. He was supposed to be at the station, but no one would think to look for him back there. The time for action had come. He placed the gun to his chin and pulled the trigger. But instead of death, he awoke moments later to intense pain. It didn't work. He was still alive.

After three hours of walking around spitting blood, he realized he needed to take a second shot. Then he started thinking about his kids, and didn't want them to think he died a long, horrible death. So he called 911 and then sat on the front porch. A fire friend showed up who'd been out looking for him, and then two more. Then the engine arrived, and everybody he knew was there. He learned later that the bullet went up through the roof of his mouth and lodged into his nasal cavity, stopping short of his brain. He was given a second chance.

In the days that followed, Bob was surprised to learn how many people actually cared about him. He went through surgery, and then spent several days in ICU. He later got help with the depression. He enrolled into a 12-step program to rid the drinking. His thoughts became clearer.

Over time, he realized there were better solutions to the problems in his life. He was grateful for the second chance. These days, he shares his story with first responders, cops, and military at the West Coast Post-Trauma Retreat. He also speaks at Alcoholics Anonymous meetings. He's been pleased to learn that his story has deterred other suicides.

In the United States, 125-150 officers commit suicide every year.[19] Each is a unique situation with a particular story. But every one of those cops was dealing with some kind of pain, whether physical, emotional, mental, spiritual, or relational. Every one of those officers lost hope in life. Every one was convinced that it was better to die than to live another day.

Life can really be very difficult. Police officers are eyewitnesses to how true this is. Our officers deal with the worst. They see injustices. They see the depravity of men and women, and how their choices hurt and even destroy those closest to them.

If our officers are not flushing these thoughts and images regularly and replacing them with positive information, their view of the world in general will be very skewed. If they are not constantly communicating and caring for you and your children, their view of us (and our view of them) will also become skewed. Add to that an unresolved soul wound (or several), there can be a loss of hope, which leads to despair.

Recently suicide hit my extended family. I listened tearfully to a loved one's cry. "I wish I would've known how he felt," she whispered. "He listened to me. Perhaps I could've helped."

Bob said that he didn't realize that something was wrong, and neither did 99.9 percent of those around him. He said there was only one co-worker who asked if he was OK about two weeks before his attempt. Of course, he lied.

We are our spouse's compass, and their backup. If we suspect something, particularly if things are not good between us, it is important to get someone else involved. It is hard to pay attention when all you're doing is arguing—but if you have that nagging feeling that won't go away, listen to it.

---

19 http://www.badgeoflife.com/currentmyths.php

What do we as spouses look for—how can we see their thoughts? Here is a list of warning signs that show an officer may be contemplating suicide:

- Excessive Drinking
- Prescription Drug Abuse
- Finances in Turmoil
- In Need of Family Counseling
- Struggling with Addiction
- Marital Issues
- Depression
- Erratic Behavior
- Loss of Interest in Job
- Suicide Attempt
- Alienation
- Changes in Weight/Appetite
- Feelings of Hopelessness
- Unable to Sleep[20]

If you suspect that your officer may be contemplating suicide, what should you do? Here are some options:

- Ask them if they are thinking about hurting themselves. This may be the one time someone asks, and it might be the one chance to intervene.
  - o If the answer is yes, do not leave the officer alone, not even for a minute. Get them help immediately.
- Take all suicidal comments, threats, or hints seriously, even jokes.
- Don't panic, and don't judge.
- Listen intently if he will talk to you.
- Do not keep this to yourself. Get help right away.
- Read your officer the next section below.
- Do not trivialize problems or tell them to "knock it off."

---

20 List from SafeCallNow.org.

- Understand his department's procedure for emergency suicide intervention. Many departments will have assistance units or peer support that are trained to help quickly and confidentially.
- If the department doesn't have resources to offer or you are wary of contacting them for whatever reason, call BlueLine Support at 855-964-2583 for guidance. They have a vast network of resources and help all over the country. It is confidential.

If You Are Contemplating Suicide

Our thoughts can be deceptive—we take facts and circumstances and filter them through our individual grids. Depending on the details and their emotional depth, our attitudes in the midst of struggles, and our inner fortitude based on upbringing/training, we come up with the conclusions all of these factors add up to in our minds. Yet our thoughts may be far from reality. This isn't necessarily mental illness—rather how our thoughts are filtered into distorted/confused arguments when we don't have all the facts. When life is overwhelming and unraveling, circumstances squeeze out answers, and the pain grows deeper still. It's difficult to want to go on. It seems relief will only come once life ends.

You may be contemplating suicide right now. Will you allow me to be a voice in your consideration? You may be listening to other voices— voices from the past that injure you, voices of anger that want to hurt you, voices that say you are worthless, and voices that deceive you into thinking there is no hope, no solution, no end to the pain you now experience.

Call BlueLine Support at 855-964-2583.

There are some things you need to know. For those who consider suicide a viable option, here is a list of consequences that actually happen. If you kill yourself:

- Your life will end on earth.
- This last act may define your legacy.
- You will wound your children, no matter what age they are, and no matter what your relationship looks like.
- You will wound your spouse, even if you are at odds right now.

- You will break your parents' hearts.
- You will hurt your friends and coworkers.
- Some will be incredibly angry with you.
- Some who love you will be embarrassed and ashamed of the way you died.
- Some will take on guilt, and it will have a painful impact on their lives.
- Some will blame themselves, even though it isn't their fault.
- Some will say you were mentally ill. You won't be around to convince them otherwise.
- You will leave a lasting horrific picture for those who find you, which will be loved ones and possibly coworkers.
- You will let depression and despair have its victory.
- You will leave unanswered questions.
- If you are leading a secret life, it will be exposed. You will not have the chance to explain, nor apologize, nor make it right.
- Your life is interconnected with others; your suicide will leave a painful void. Even in people you wouldn't have guessed.

As desperate and hopeless as things may seem, consider:

- Though you may not see it now, there is hope. Hope in love, hope in healing, hope in changes you can make in your life. Until you pull the trigger, it isn't too late to seek a different course of action.
- Though you may feel alone, you are not. Call out to others you trust even a little.
- If you are hearing voices that say you are worthless and you shouldn't be alive, this is a lie. The truth is that God gave you life with purpose and value.
- If you are weary of life, perhaps try something new—something selfless, something meaningful, something healthy.
- Depression is a symptom of unaddressed hurts and unresolved anger. It is a curable condition.
- Post-Traumatic Stress is a reality that thousands of military, civilians, peace officers, firemen, and first responders are dealing with right this *minute*. Bad things happened, and you witnessed it. You

need to know that it's okay to feel awful about a horrible situation. It is a normal response to an abnormal event(s), and there are solutions to PTS(D). Talk to someone who's been there. Call BlueLine Support at 855-964-2583.

- Life is a series of ups and downs. If this is a particularly bad season, give it time and connect with others. They will help you through it.
- Don't end your life in defeat—live your life strong! Understand your weaknesses as well as your strengths and accept both. There are those who love you, and those that need you. Don't let them down.

The Fight Against Losing Hope

These last three chapters have been difficult ones, and I hope that you and your officer don't have a need to reread them—ever. But this crisis-driven career and its challenges can be overwhelming at times. There will be times when you will have to fight for your marriage, fight for your officer, and maybe fight against losing hope.

Brent and I had a three-year period in our marriage in which we had several very difficult issues that stacked themselves against us. We had some serious family concerns, health scares, financial challenges, conflicts, losses, and endured a season of his career like he'd never experienced before. There were days I pushed the grocery cart in the store thinking, "I can't do this!" It was a fight to just to stay in the game.

Now that we are on the other side of that very dark season, I have thought a lot about how we survived, and what we have learned.

Know Your Enemies and Your Allies, Then Arm Yourself

Since Ferguson, it is very clear that police families have enemies. The anti-police sentiments and lies that are treated as fact come to mind. But I have found that people are not really the enemy. It is ideas and attitudes and that people *carry* that are the enemies. And the ones that creep into our homes are the worst.

Take **negativity**, for example. It's all around us. Accusations, rumors, half-truths, opinions, and blame are riddled with negativity. Negativity is a thief that steals joy, clarity and courage. How do we respond? We can fan its flame by joining in, offering excuses, names, rebuttals, our differing opinions, and blame right back. I have seen Facebook posts from cop wives that are vulgar retaliations; spewing the same kind of anger and hatred they are firing back at. It only fans the flame of negativity, causing it to burn out of control.

We can take it in and let it fester, growing in resentment. This is hard not to do—because it's so discouraging. I've been guilty of this, so finally I had to close my computer and avoid it all. That was a good decision.

If we can't avoid it, we can take that stuff and flush it—the truth is what matters, and what we hear most are opinions, assumptions, and interpretations that may or may not be based on fact, not necessarily the truth.

We also fight negativity with positive wisdom. We have to remember where this stuff comes from—considering the source and their agendas. If we can calmly and rationally speak into it and give different perspectives, we should. But if negativity is so entrenched that folks just won't listen, it's better to leave them be.

Complacency is an enemy as well. We can be inactive, reactive, or proactive in the way we do life. If we're not careful, we can allow ourselves to lose interest, or go through the motions without really caring. Complacency is a clever enemy that slips in unnoticed while we adhere to our routines. We're busy with lots of activity, putting off things that really matter like exercise, time off, intimacy, and then—WHAM!—we are broadsided. Complacency kills.

We fight complacency with priorities and boundaries. We have to be intentional, making choices that protect our minds, our marriage, and our kids. We can't push the accelerator all the time, nor can we put the brakes on all the time. It's a combination of the two, directed by what we truly desire to happen in our lives.

Fear and **worry** are the enemy twins, digging holes in the soul and wreaking havoc with our decisions. They are slave masters, conjuring up irrational imaginations and then shackling them to our souls. This enemy will not allow room for progress.

We combat fear and worry with faith (see chapter five). Faith in the things that are real and trustworthy.

Lastly, **isolation**—the enemy that erects thick walls around us and then attacks from within. Isolation separates us to allow all other enemies to flood in and feast, devouring uninhibited the clarity that comes only through others.

We combat isolation with connection with family and friends. We cannot fight against these enemies alone. In the Disney movie *Jungle Book*, Mowgli has wandered away from sleeping Bagheera, and is met by Kaa, a hungry snake. He slithers and hums and dances, hypnotizing Mowgli into his clutches, seeking to squeeze and devour him. It almost works until Bagheera wakes up, bops the snake on the head, and rescues Mowgli. When Kaa turns his hypnotizing attentions to Bagheera, Mowgli returns the rescue favor, and Kaa is forced to move on. This scene is a great picture of how others can save us from the hypnotizing effects of isolation. Other perspectives serve as a bop on the head—bringing negative thoughts closer to the truth.

We need others in our camp to give us another perspective—one that protects, clarifies, and prevents enemies from getting the upper hand. Allies who will go to battle for our hearts and minds and marriage. Allies who will come alongside and walk through all seasons of our lives.

Discussion Group Questions

1. Am I practicing good emotional care in my life? Is my officer?
2. Do I suspect my officer has struggled with suicidal thoughts?
3. Have I had to fight any of the enemies mentioned? Others?
4. Who was my ally in that fight? How did this ally come to your rescue?

CHAPTER 10
PEEPS AND PROPS: YOUR SUPPORT SYSTEM

It started with a funeral… All of our husbands had to work it, so several of us went to Chili's, ate chocolate cake, and cried together. We've been close ever since.

FAYE, CALIFORNIA

Have someone on the outside to be a sounding board, have ten more on the inside to be a support system, and be prepared to learn how to do a lot on your own.

SARAH, PENNSYLVANIA

Have a backup spouse for events that yours can't attend. Keep your friends who are not part of the LE family close. They keep an amazing balance in your life. Find a few new and experienced LE spouses to connect with. They are the only ones who understand what you're going through. They will also be up late worrying when there is a situation…

LUANA, CALIFORNIA

It was a mix and match evening. There were cops' wives who were married from three to thirty-two years. There were different departments, nationalities, ages, and viewpoints. We had a former dispatcher, a wife who had two sons on the force, and two wives of retired policemen. Several had gone through critical incidents and the aftermath with their husbands. Some had gone through struggles in their marriages and almost didn't make it. And yet the unity was undeniable. Those who'd never met before were hugging and exchanging numbers by the end of the night.

I hadn't expected this when I invited several wives of law enforcement to my home to talk about our lives. I was pleasantly surprised at their insight; heads nodded around the table as each took a turn to describe what being a wife of a law enforcement officer was like. At the end of the evening, several women said that even though they'd never done something like this, they wanted to do it again and soon.

I learned something that night. No matter our differences, we need each other.

A Need Indeed!

We have so many demands on our time. Work, children, and managing our homes consume hours and energy. Add to that a husband's crisis-driven career, and there's not a lot of time for much else. We can live our lives moving from task to task, and there is a certain amount of satisfaction with this. But after awhile, loneliness sets in. We need connection. We need to laugh together, cry together. We need someone to hear the fifty thousand words we have to get out every day. And our kids just can't meet these needs.

The California Highway Patrol Academy holds two important events for every cadet class. The day before the cadets report for training, the staff hosts a family orientation seminar. The purpose is to educate loved ones as to what their cadet will go through and suggest ways to help them through the next twenty-seven weeks. The day before graduation, family members of those graduating are invited to a family support panel. The purpose of this meeting is to educate families for their first steps as an officer. In both events seasoned wives are invited to encourage, validate, and connect with other families. Swapping numbers with nearby people, encouraging Facebook connections online, and grouping families according to geographical area of assignment is a big part of the connection process. The reason our department does this is that they have recognized the importance of support systems for our officers and their families. It is becoming increasingly apparent that LEO families need to have connection with and support from those who love them. Their emotional survival depends on it.

You and I are no different. We may be the support systems for our men in uniform, but we can't do it alone either. When we deal with what comes home, we need validation of our thoughts and actions. It is good to get feedback from those we trust, and most of all we need healthy doses of encouragement that come from others who love us. Living life together gives us confidence and security.

Let's start with you as an individual. Do you have close friends or family who support you, your marriage, and your kids? Chances are you have a great support system in place. But what if your husband's job takes you to another part of the state or country? Or you have a strained relationship with your mother? Or your spouse just started his career in law enforcement and your friends not only don't understand but also don't want to?

Brent and I have lived in several parts of our state as he's transferred for promotions. My experience is that I have been the one to take the initiative in making friends. In southern California, before I had children, my workplace was where I found my friends. I found myself tagging along with single girls when Brent was working or looked forward to ladies' nights out with coworkers. We went to the Hollywood Bowl together, threw wedding and baby showers, and went to lunch. I learned a lot about LA's creative variety hanging out with these gals.

Once I had children, it seemed to be a little easier to find friends. I joined a local Mothers of Preschoolers chapter and got involved. I was invited by another CHP wife and loved it. As the kids grew older, I met ladies at school functions and the gym. We'd work out and then go to coffee afterward for girl time.

One of my closest friends is a young woman who moved to Sacramento the same time I did, and we met in a Bible study. Once I learned her husband was with the Air Force and they lived five minutes away, our families began living our lives together almost every day. We have continued to keep in touch through the years and spend many of our vacations visiting them in whatever state they reside.

One question I hear often from new officers' wives is, "How do I get in touch with other law enforcement wives?" It's not as easy as it might seem. Sometimes you just have to extend an invitation for coffee without expectations. You never know whom you'll connect with and whom you won't. With the friend in the Air Force, I had to ask her several times to get together before she actually took me up on it. She and her husband weren't used to getting to know people much because they moved often. We cured them of that.

Annie's husband, Tim, was with county homicide. It was hard on him, and he wasn't the same person after he saw some awful things. I asked her how she dealt with it. She told me that in addition to her church, she has some great friends in law enforcement. She had grown close to a female deputy who was also married to an officer. When their husbands worked swing shift, they would take the kids out to have some fun. Sometimes they got home just before their husbands did! But Annie told me that those fun times were what got her and the kids through those long, lonely evenings.

Another thing that works fairly well within offices is to get groups of wives together on a regular basis, grass-roots style. The best example I've seen is what my friend Faye put together. She and a couple of ladies started going to coffee together. Then they went to a play. Soon they invited more and more ladies from the station to join them, and they came up with a variety of monthly events. Faye had the vision to connect the women in her husband's office, and she went for it. It caught on. Then when one of the women's husbands was killed in the line of duty, they stepped up and took care of her, comforting her and meeting practical needs. It was community they created, and it naturally kicked into action when crisis hit. Faye and I are now actively encouraging others to do the same thing in other areas of California.

A couple years after the first edition of CHiP on my Shoulder came out, I put out some feelers online and with friends to meet together and go through it together. We had an amazing 13 weeks together, and we learned a lot about each other and ourselves. We took turns bringing baked goodies and had lots of coffee. Those girls were amazing. A few months after we were done with the book, tragedy struck our area. Because the incident included several departments, I checked to make sure everyone's husband was okay. It turned out that several of our husbands were involved, and one of us who was a dispatcher. As we went through roll call, we learned that one of our husbands was actually at the original incident and had experienced major trauma. Some of us from the group were able to come alongside our friend, and we've become even closer.

Another way that we've seen great connection on a larger level is groups of law enforcement wives online. Our cadet wives have been creating small groups on Facebook. This is a great way to keep in touch with several people at once and when you don't live close to other wives. This is an incredible way to gain information, ask questions about benefits, support families through critical incidents and family emergencies, and just toss out ideas. When face-to-face isn't always available, this is a great way to connect.

There are some things to consider, however. There is etiquette that has developed over the years that we should adhere to, and boundaries that will protect our families.

Guidelines for Social Media

- Conduct yourself online like you would in person—you never know who's watching, or who they're connected to.
- When posting articles, remember who your friends are.
- Never post or share nude or compromising photos of yourself online—they're not private, and they can turn up anywhere.
- Remember your tone can be misinterpreted online depending on the words you use.
- Never post personal and identifying information on public pages—always send a message.
- When a critical incident happens, hold off saying ANYTHING on the group page until you are positive the information has been released by the department. Too many wives find out about tragic accidents or loss of their husbands online. If your husband shares information with you, keep it to yourself. Do not contact survivors until you are sure that they have been notified.
- Do not threaten people.

- If you have a beef with someone on a group page, contact that person directly. Don't be *that girl* who drudges up drama for all to see.
- Ask permission to post photos—don't assume it's okay.

Girls Are Mean!

I ran into an acquaintance that I hadn't seen in awhile. We quickly caught each other up on our families, and she mentioned that her nine-year-old daughter was giving her fits. I nodded. "That's when their hormones start up," I shared. "I bet she's also experiencing drama with other girls at school, isn't she?" She looked at me like I was psychic. I went on to recall stories of my girls when they turned that magic number nine. It was a hurtful time; girls were so mean!

Sometimes interacting with other women is scary. We've all been there at some time or another—some girl is creating drama, and suddenly *connection* isn't such a hot idea. The good news is as we mature, there are fewer of us who take part in this kind of stuff. But definitely not all, and I'll be honest—cop wives can be really tough. That's why I say, "Proceed with caution!" If you find yourself connecting with a woman who is gossiping, run—don't walk—to the nearest exit. Even if she's talking trash about someone you don't like, chances are she'll eventually talk trash about you too.

Rules of Engagement

Over the years I have worked with, served, taught, mentored, spoke to, and counseled hundreds of women of all backgrounds. I've learned through trial and error how to be a friend and observed those that do friendship well. I've come up with some general rules of engagement that will help you pick some good friends and be a good friend in return.

The Number-One Golden Rule

I'll start with the most basic. We learned this in school or from our moms early on, but it represents a very good boundary for our behavior! The golden rule is to do to others what you would have them do to you. If you want someone to keep your secrets, keep hers. If kindness is important to you, then be kind. If you would like some practical help here and there, then offer and follow through with practical help. Fill in the blanks from there.

Keep this in mind as you converse with others. As women, we have a tendency to talk too much. Oh, the words we say, every day, in lots of ways! But we all have two ears and one mouth. Listening is twice as important as talking. Ooh, this is a good reminder for me! I have so many stories, and I like to tell those stories to make connections to this and that—show others how much we have in common! But I like to be listened to, so I have had to teach myself to shut my mouth and listen.

Rule Number Two: What's the Backstory?

Novelists are always on the lookout for creative ways to bring in the backstory. This is the prelude to what you're reading in the book, the reasons or the road to how the character got where they are physically and emotionally in the story. The same goes for real people; there's *always* a backstory.

I have learned to never make assumptions based on first impressions. Some women are shy. Some women want to be friends, but want to first observe if you're trustworthy or not. When I speak, it's often the women who don't make eye contact with me during my talk that approach me afterwards to ask questions.

You'd be surprised how many women are carrying burdens that come across as indifference to others. Those who come across as confident, engaged women can actually be harboring feelings of self-doubt just beneath the surface.

Things aren't always as they appear. We don't always have the facts. That fabulously dressed brunette sitting by herself with a don't-approach-me look has a story. She probably isn't stuck up. She probably doesn't think she's better than you. She might be shy. Or she was abused as a child. Or she and her husband had an argument on the way there. Or she has ten dollars in her bank account and no groceries in the fridge. You never know what is behind the blank stare or the up front attitude. But it might be worth it to try to find out the backstory. It just might be very similar to your own.

Rule Number Three: They Are One, Not Two

Rose's husband is a deputy with a nearby county sheriff's department. She was recounting to me how the office had experienced severe drama in the last several months, and it was wearing on her even though she wasn't directly involved. There were two people having an affair at the office—an officer who was married and the wife of another deputy. Everyone knew except the spouses, and they were all trying to keep it a secret while gossiping about it. What a mess.

You will socialize with other attractive men in uniforms throughout your husband's career. Chances are your friends' husbands are nice to look at too. But if we are to conduct ourselves in a way that makes us safe friends, we must establish boundaries with other men.

I have developed a defense mechanism against letting handsome men get into my thoughts. When I see a married man who is attractive, I make sure to meet his wife. Then I look at them as one entity, not two. When I see Robert, I see Sue. When I see Scott, I see Lisa. This has worked for me; it keeps my mind in check. Looking at them as a couple keeps me from flirting and therefore doesn't stir up bad vibes with my friends. The friendships keep me accountable. I don't even go there, and others sense that I'm trustworthy.

I also have to mention the way we dress. Women are beautiful. And how we clothe ourselves makes a big statement to others about who we are and what we value. Dressing to attract (very short skirts, low-cut tops, ultra tight pants) may get the attention of men, but it screams to other women that they can't trust her. She's unsafe, threatening. Dressing nicely but appropriately helps other women trust you as a friend.

Rule Number Four: Loose Lips Sink Ships!

Have you ever poured a bag of sugar into a canister and realized too late that it wasn't big enough to hold the whole bag? There are sugar crystals everywhere! They're on the counter, the floor, and your clothes. You can sweep for the next three days and still feel them on your shoes.

This is what happens when we don't use discretion. Once your words are out of the bag, they can end up anywhere.

Within departments there are always politics. I can't tell you how many times key people have tried to get me to talk about my views on things. They've tried to get information. I am learning to keep my opinions to myself because my views will be read as my husband's views. And that could get him into hot water.

When you are socializing with people from the department, play out beforehand what you will disclose and not disclose. You don't ever have to be rude unless someone gets out of line. Smile. But be careful about passing along information that could jeopardize the well being of your husband. Better yet, stay clear of controversial work topics and share about the other aspects of your lives.

Rule Number Five: No Comparison!

I used to be very intimidated by women who were perfectly dressed, not a hair out of place, makeup just so, and who had expensive taste. Such a person attended a bridal shower at my home. She took a look around the rooms of my home. She was restless. The way it seemed, she was looking down her nose at me. Even my daughter was uncomfortable with the way she asked questions. Years ago I would've immediately been insecure and projected my perceived flaws into her brain. *I'm not as pretty as she. She probably noticed the rip in that chair. She probably noticed I didn't mop the floor before everyone got there. She probably thinks I could lose a few pounds. I could stand to lose a few pounds. I should reconsider my wrinkle cream. I need a new chair...*

Have you been there? Why do we do this to ourselves? Why do we compare and then decide we're inferior or better than another woman? What is that?

Could it be that we subscribe to the Mirror, Mirror on the Wall Thing? What a bunch of hoopla. You have value. I have value. That value is not mutually exclusive. It is mutually *inclusive*. Women were the crowning glory of God's creation—we were created to be beautiful—let's embrace our value, and see the value in other women as well.

Someone Older and Wiser

Renee's husband, Joel, had been deployed to Iraq twice. When his time was up with the National Guard, he went to work for the sheriff's department. Renee had struggled deeply with little kids in tow while he was in the Middle East. She felt very alone, and there wasn't much support available. Those years were very hard. So when Joel came home and became a cop, she was glad that he was home, but there were still stresses with his job.

About that time she met a woman who was also a deputy wife. Cyndi was a little older, and her husband had been with the county for several years. She took a liking to Renee, and they soon found they had much in common. Soon this friendship blossomed into a mentoring relationship. Cyndi called Renee from time to time and asked her how she was faring. She'd answer questions and listened to Renee's concerns. She gently guided Renee to keep on investing in her marriage and children and offered understanding and helpful ideas. Unlike the lonely deployment experience, she felt supported and strong.

I, too, have benefited from mentoring relationships. When I was younger, I sought out confident women that I respected and asked them to meet with me for guidance. The time was invaluable. I sat soaking in tried and true wisdom and remember much of what they said all these years later.

In recent years I have been able to pay it forward. I now mentor several cop wives from all over the country and feel honored that younger women want to meet with/call me. I love listening and sharing wisdom and asking questions to get them to really think about the deep stuff.

If this kind of a friendship appeals to you, start looking for a seasoned woman from the office or another department. It helps if she is a law enforcement wife, but it doesn't have to necessarily be so. Look for a wise, quiet yet confident woman who cares about you and your marriage. Then take the plunge and ask her to meet for coffee.

From My Heart to Yours: My Faith

In this day and age, it's a little taboo to talk about your faith. But I would be remiss if I didn't share with you the most important person in my support system: God. Now I'm not talking about regular attendance at church, although I love my church and am involved there. I'm not talking about religion, which in my mind conjures up a list of requirements we need to do or not do to be accepted or get into heaven. I'm talking about an actual relationship with God, walking and talking with Him in every aspect of my life. I meet Him for coffee every morning, pouring out my heart (praying) about things I'm concerned about, and then searching the Bible for answers. Sometimes I actually hear His still, small voice.

I did the religious thing growing up. It was about adhering to a set of rules that basically removed a lot of "fun" from life. In my teens I'd had enough—so rebelled heavily against my parents and their Christian values. I soon found myself pretty broken, used, angry, and had lost the beauty of my innocence. The "fun" wasn't actually fun at all. I turned to Jesus Christ humbly and desperately, asking that He clean me up from my mistakes and help me make better choices. I didn't receive judgment, I found grace and forgiveness. He responded by telling me that I was forgiven, cleansed, and actually a new person, because He paid the penalties for what I'd done on the cross over 2000 years ago. He had plans for my life; plans that would bring healing to my soul, change my heart and character into someone who deeply cared for others, and then become all that He saw I could be.

I'm now living in that freedom. Though it isn't always easy following Jesus, and it certainly isn't popular anymore, I have indescribable joy in the journey and hope for my future.

As far as this journey as a cop wife, God has met my needs when my husband couldn't. I am fully loved by God, and this gives me security and inner joy. I can make peace with my weaknesses, because I have help from Him in the times I fall short. I depend on Him to take care of my family, including when Brent is at risk. Best of all, I am never alone. He's only a whisper away, giving me what I need at any given moment.

So, this is the secret to my strength as a woman and as a cop's wife. For some of you this is very familiar, but for others, foreign. If you'd like to hear more, contact me via my website. I *will* get back to you.

Your Spouse!

Up to this point I have talked about getting support from others. But I cannot move ahead without mentioning the most influential person of your support system: your spouse! You are one entity, and you can lean on one another. Two lives intertwined, investing time, resources, and parts of yourselves to build a life together.

A long-term marriage is a journey of growth. I mentioned earlier that Brent and I had spent our earlier years peeling off our rough edges so that we can enjoy our soft centers in the later years. To be able to do this takes a two-way give and take, not a one-sided approach. Some of your needs will only be met by him.

Your spouse's input and support is valuable no matter how hard it may be to hear. Our officers many times will be brutally honest; they've been trained to call it like they see it. For many of us, this is hard to take.

Kim didn't see James as her protector for many years. Every time she brought her unresolved conflicts to him from work, he'd ask questions about her response. He was never quick to join her pity parties and didn't seem to take her side much. He was painfully objective. After awhile Kim translated that to mean that he didn't care enough to protect her.

But James had a different approach. His support was unwavering for Kim, but he had a whole-picture viewpoint. Rather than take her side no matter what, he thought it best to counsel her to see the situation not as a victim but as an involved party. Sometimes Kim would be right, but not always. James felt she should take responsibility for her part in problems, not just enable the victim mentality she resorted to. As Kim matured over the years, she came to see that James was no doubt a protector—he protected her dignity.

Your spouse can support you even if he doesn't see things your way. In fact, it is always better to get another opinion that is different from your own and then think it through. Our officers are trained to ask good questions and think objectively. Generally women are led by compassion and empathy as well as a healthy need for significance. But these strong emotions can sometimes trick us. We may not be able to see the full picture. Our husbands can add in other thoughts that help balance us out, and vice versa. They are a strong addition to our support system.

Reinforcements

Sometimes we need a little help to get past the obstacles we face in our marriages. Finding other people who can help you in some way is another piece of your support system. Mentoring and marriage retreats can be a great way to invest in your relationship, as can counseling.

Erica and Marlo, mentioned in previous chapters, go to counseling regularly, like dental check ups. They need a little cleaning to keep things healthy. Others go only when they are in crisis. But do your homework. Not all counselors are created equal. Try to get some recommendations. Inquire if they work with law enforcement. If you are of a particular faith, you may want to ensure that the counselor's approach is compatible with your beliefs. Spend time in the research beforehand and have their information available for when you need it.

Counsel, friendships with women, God, your relationship with your spouse, and other members of law enforcement all make up your support system. You can't do life alone and remain healthy. We need each other for the ups and for the downs.

Discussion Group Questions

1. Who is the one who supports you the best? Give an example.
2. Which of the four rules of friendship did you like to see? Why?
3. Has faith in God been a part of your support system? How?
4. Spend the rest of your time brainstorming some events that you all would like to do together.

CHAPTER 11
SILVER BULLETS: MONEY AND YOUR MARRIAGE

Treat overtime pay as an extra. Do no set up your financial life to be dependent upon it.
MICHELLE, CALIFORNIA

Don't even consider keeping up with the Joneses. THEY'RE BROKE!
DAVE RAMSEY, FINANCIAL ADVISOR

It's no secret. Across the country and beyond, we're vulnerable to economic trends. Why? Because, for most of us, we are dependent upon other people's money. We have become increasingly dependent on Wall Street, banks, and the government. We work hard, and then everyone takes a cut. Then we get to choose how to spend the leftovers. If we decide that the leftovers aren't enough, we borrow. Pretty soon our choices are made for us; we no longer have enough left over from the leftovers to live. It's a vicious cycle, and we've seen the consequences of this in the last few years. People are losing their homes, jobs, and more. Cop families are no different.

Carl and Tina declared bankruptcy and lost their gorgeous house because they bought whatever they wanted on credit and then couldn't pay the mortgage.

Quinn and Saul both work just to make ends meet because half of Saul's salary goes to alimony payments.

Brian and Marcy depended on his overtime to make their house payment. It severely cut back Brian's opportunities to expand professionally, and he was hardly home with his family.

Carrie and Andy bought an expensive house on the outreaches of what they could afford. Then the police department implemented a pay cut. She ended up having to teach school when she desperately wanted to be home with her little girls.

All of these families are law enforcement. Good careers. Excellent benefits. Decent salaries. But no matter how much money is made, failure to plan is a plan for failure.

The Role of Hypervigilance

There are law enforcement-related issues that affect our money. Hypervigilance and critical incident stress have their effects. Dr. Gilmartin says,

> The behavioral and marketing researchers on Madison Avenue have... clearly established that certain individuals, when feeling mildly depressed or unfocused, can find themselves feeling more energetic if they purchase something. This form of "retail therapy" does have distinct gender differences. Women tend to make small ticket purchases... Males do not appear to like to go shopping, but they do enjoy "buying stuff"... big-ticket items like boats, cars, pickup trucks, motor homes, campers, and maybe some power tools.[21]

What happens is that retail therapy can turn into debt. And debt becomes a huge burden that results in extra jobs and overtime. The catch phrase he who has the most toys wins turns into he who has the most toys whines.

This spending pattern affects our marriages. More and more debt is added to our limited resources and can rob us of financial security. We are constantly behind, working harder and harder to catch up.

One of the benefits of police work is the financial security it brings to the family. Most sworn police officers are in it for the long haul; a twenty-to-thirty year career in law enforcement is the goal. There are exceptions, but depending on what your department offers in pay and benefits, chances are good that you'll belong to the middle class. Also,

21 Kevin Gilmartin, *Emotional Survival for Law Enforcement*, (Tuscon, Arizona: E-S Press, 2002) pages 128-129.

law enforcement is a reasonably secure profession. There will always be crime; therefore, we will always need police officers.

But if we allow ourselves to get into debt to the point that we are strapped financially, that feeling of security begins to wane. When our officers are working day in and day out but money is constantly coming up short, a sense of frustration can develop. These feelings will heap on top of regular pressures of the job, and can lead to a feeling of desperation. At this point, talking about money will become very difficult.

Money Talks

Ted and Sarah have difficulty talking about money, as it is a constant source of conflict. Ted gets frustrated that he works hard to bring in the money and they never seem to get ahead. Sarah naturally avoids conflict, so she inadvertently sabotages their efforts by not communicating with Ted about upcoming bills. This of course angers Ted and adds late charges to an already tight budget.

Even though money seems like it should be handled without emotion, it isn't. So much of who we are is wrapped up in our money! For men the traditional role as provider says a lot about who they are as a man. The expectations have been built up into status. If you make a lot of money, you are a success. If you don't, not so much.

For women, we tend to view money as security. If we have money, we don't have to worry about where to live, what we wear, and what we eat. If we are short on money, we tend to worry.

Rich and Anna didn't have a large income, but they made it work. However, Rich felt that because he worked hard he deserved a nice truck. He spent a lot of money on his trucks while Anna scrimped and saved and did odd jobs to feed and clothe the kids. Over the years Anna and Rich had many arguments, and eventually Anna took over the management of the money. She didn't give Rich much to spend, so when Rich got an overtime check, he'd cash it and spend it without telling her.

How you handle money can build trust or be a source of mistrust. Typically, every couple has a spender and a saver. And unless the two have agreed upon goals and budgets, the constant push and pull of the money can be destructive to a marriage. The solution lies in acknowledging our shortcomings and for both to be involved in money management. We need to ask ourselves the hard questions and then answer honestly:

- Who is the saver, who is the spender?
- What are our individual responsibilities?
- What do we both want from our money?
- Are we both committed to improving this area?
- Where can we cut our spending to invest in our future?
- When do we waver in our control of spending?
- How did we get ourselves into the debt we have? How will we get out?
- Are we a slave to our home, striving to make the payments?
- Is our money working for us, or against us?
- How deep are we willing to cut luxuries to ease financial stress?

Have a regular business meeting with your husband to get on top of things. When we are proactive about communicating, especially when it comes to money, it will have an accumulating effect much like the emotional bank account. For the one who does most of the money business, it'll really help him/you feel a lighter burden.

To keep our money life intact, we need some guiding principles. Then we need a plan based on those principles. I've included some financial guidelines that Brent and I have learned and tried to practice over the years.

Keep Your Money Life Intact

- Spend less than you earn. This should be a no-brainer, but most people just don't adhere to this idea. When I was a newlywed, my boss told me, "You should live on Brent's salary and save yours." I thought he was nuts. But I will tell you it was the best advice we never followed. Had we taken his advice, we would've been in much better shape early on.
- Debt is a burden you can choose not to carry. When we don't save and pay cash for items other than a mortgage, we will pay

much more for what we buy. Sales prices will quickly be added to in a hurry. Why do you think we get discounts for using credit at department stores? The odds are in their favor that we won't be able to pay it off before we incur interest.

- Budget, budget, budget! This is the only way we can live within our means. We have found that the best way to do this is through a software program. There are many programs from which to choose. Do a Google search and you'll have more information than you ever dreamed. We have successfully used Quicken for years, but there are other programs that may offer options that are better suited to your taste. We can pay bills, budget, keep track of what we spend, and even download our spending into TurboTax, making tax time just a little easier.
- The 10-10-80 spending plan. Ten percent goes to savings. Ten percent goes toward giving to charity. Budget and spend the rest. My daughter is excellent at this plan. When she started babysitting at twelve years of age, she put together a spreadsheet on the computer that charted her progress. She's been faithful to it ever since. She gave 10 percent to our church and other needy causes, then put 60 percent into her savings, and spent 30 percent on fun stuff. She was able to do this because we were taking care of her needs. Once she became an adult and is now taking on more financial responsibility, she has new percentages that include her car and school expenses, but even now she still gives 10 percent to charity and 20 percent to savings.
- Don't spend; invest. Typically we look at money as something we spend rather than a tool used to invest in our futures. When we have this slightly different perspective, we tend to be more proactive in proceeding wisely with our money. When we have goals and dreams for our futures and then view our money as the means to meet them, we are much less likely to let our money slip through our fingers.

It *Can* Be Better

Are we destined to always struggle with our money? How much is enough? Will there ever be enough? Like Ted, does your husband feel the pressure of providing for the family yet feel as if the debt gets bigger as the hopes grow smaller to ever reach your goals? If so you're not alone. Unlike most relational things, there actually is a formula to solve our financial woes.

I once heard two cop wives talking about their finances. They were both on the same money plan and were comparing notes.

"Where are you in the process?" asked Barbara.

"We are now debt-free, except for the mortgage," Eve said with a smile.

"Wow! That was quick!"

"We had a lot of things to sell," explained Eve, "Then we took the money and paid off debt. We found a renter for our big house, and now we have a down payment on a smaller home in a better community. It's all been working out very well. We don't have to count on Ben's overtime anymore. How about you?"

"We have about a year and a half, and we'll be debt free. We've whittled our expenses down to the point that we have extra money each month that goes toward paying off our credit cards. It is so freeing!"

The plan that Barbara and Eve were speaking of is Dave Ramsay's "Total Money Makeover." His book of the same name shares a simple yet smart plan to get out of debt as soon as possible and then use your money to build wealth in smart ways. Brent and I took a money class shortly after we were married. The class was called *Master Your Money*, by Ron Blue. We learned some great principles for managing our finances. More recently we read Ramsay's book together. His ideas and principles were very timely.

Whether you choose Dave Ramsay, Ron Blue, or something else, the point is to have an agreed upon plan. If you are currently in a difficult place financially, there is hope. Get creative. It's amazing to watch your money make the shift from burden to delight as you get spending under control and see it grow. It'll be one more thing under control in your law enforcement life. And that makes a huge difference!

Bonus!

Once our oldest daughter was born, I quit work and stayed home with our children. It was reducing to one income that forced us to pinch pennies.

We had mouths to feed and only so much money to buy that food. I've listed some ways that we have implemented to bring down our costs.

- Get out of debt; interest should be the first expense to go.
- Pay your bills on time; late fees should not be a budget item.
- Have your paycheck direct deposited; many times banks will waive a monthly service charge if you do this. Credit unions usually do not charge bank fees for accounts.
- Raise your insurance deductibles as high as you can comfortably go; this will bring down your premiums. Then make sure you have the deductible in savings.
- Turn off the lights when you leave the room, unplug appliances after use, and turn off computers at night. Use extra freezers or refrigerators only when entertaining.
- Shop at discount stores and warehouses. Split large quantities with friends.
- Go without meat a couple of nights a week for dinner. Have pasta with marinara or salads or soups. Rice and beans are a great supper with complete protein and no expensive cuts of meat.
- Buy juice from a can and mix in your own water. You can save as much as 150 percent on the cost.
- You would be surprised at the beautiful clothes you can find at thrift shops. I have several friends who dress beautifully from thrift shop deals. You'd never know.
- If you're an avid reader, borrow fiction from the library or friends or buy used books. Only buy books new that you will refer to again (like this book). Better yet, purchase a Kindle, Nook, or iPad; ebooks are cheaper, sometimes even free.
- Cut back on newspapers and magazine subscriptions. Renew only those you read regularly. Listen to news on the radio; you can multitask, and it's free! You can also get more news than you could possibly want online for free
- Make your own coffee. Buy the good stuff: it's still cheaper to make.
- Make your own lunch. Buy the good deli meat: it's still cheaper to make.

- Make sure you don't buy extra roadside assistance if your auto insurance already offers this.
- Grow a garden. Nowadays gardens can even be grown in pots on the patio.
- Do indoor dates with homemade popcorn, a movie, and a glass of wine after the kids have gone to bed. You'll save a small fortune and won't drink and drive.
- Use coupons for restaurants!
- Eat less. This obviously doesn't apply to everyone, but for most of us, we eat more than we should. Eat only when you're hungry, and stop when you start to feel full. Share meals at restaurants with other family members instead of everyone getting their own—we just don't need the large portions most restaurants serve.
- Rather than eat in, take it to go. You save on drinks and the tip doesn't have to be as large. Have the kids share entrees to cut down on waste.
- Do your shopping on the Internet; there are always better prices. Watch for waived shipping costs and sales to get the best possible deal. Brent pays a yearly fee for two-day shipping through Amazon.com. Saves us plenty.
- Use cash instead of swiping the card—it's much harder to part with.
- Look for bundle packages on media. Cell phone service, cable, and landline service companies will sometimes work together to reduce your monthly bills.
- Make your own cleaners—they're natural and cheaper. Look online for recipes.
- Rent boats, jet skis, and other toys rather than buy. Storage fees and upkeep costs must more than you plan for, and most of the time you won't use these items as much as you think.
- If you have teenagers, pay the monthly flat rate for texting and data. It'll save you money, guaranteed. And it'll save on your minutes.
- Dollar stores offer a lot of items for cheap—soap, pregnancy tests, gift bags and wrap, greeting cards, cleaners, balloons, baskets, glasses and toys among others.

- Buying in bulk can save money—just make sure you do the math first and plan to actually use what you buy. If this is a problem, co-op with another family.
- Always ask your husband if he knows coworkers with side businesses. Cops will many times give cops a good deal. It's kind of a co-op thing. Our friend Ty has "gotta guy" for everything. When we need something done, we always ask Ty because he's already done the research.
- Inquire whether your union has concierge services. You can save money on vacations and amusement parks among other things.

These are some of the savings I have found when trying to balance the budget. They are tried and true.

Money is a huge issue for marriages, and finances have taken their toll on many families. But we can take control of this area of our marriages and make it what it needs to be. When we make the choice to keep spending under control, everyone benefits, including our children.

Discussion Group Questions

1. Brainstorm some ways to save money.
2. What is your biggest issue with money?
3. What is your greatest victory?
4. Just an idea—ya'll are coming to the end of this book. Maybe you could take a financial class together?

CHAPTER 12

LITTLE FUTURE COPS

Our three-year-old son has fully embraced the life of an LEO kid. He calls police cars Daddy Cars and will arrest me or pull me over when we are playing in the house. He actually wrote me a speeding ticket this afternoon for chasing him too fast. He will pretend like he is going to work and will fill up his backpack, grab his pretend car keys, give me a kiss, and say he is off to work. When asked where he works at, he replies, "The jail. Just like Daddy."

MEGAN, CALIFORNIA

Ask them, tell them, make them: it works on the street, but not at home.

UNKNOWN POLICE SPOUSE

I felt a little left out when my son became a patrolman. Suddenly he and my husband had their own little language and a camaraderie. When your kids go into law enforcement, it's a whole different ball game.

TRICIA, CALIFORNIA

It was a beautiful day at the park. The Easter egg hunt was over, but not all the eggs were found, so the older kids were searching the deep grass. Hot dogs sizzled on the grill. A couple of the dads were marveling together at how well the day was going.

"The kids are so well-behaved. I think it's because we don't let them get out of hand. They know if they misbehave, we'll clobber them!" said one officer, laughing.

Heads nodded in agreement because we understood; most cops' kids are held to a pretty high standard. Their dads have seen what happens out there on the street, and they don't want their kids to become *customers*. Chances are that if someone else heard this conversation, they might get the wrong idea. With all of the confusion about parenting these days, there are mixed messages about what is acceptable and not acceptable. But law enforcement parents tend to lean toward a stricter standard.

What's It Like To Be a Cop's Kid?

Cops' kids generally don't get away with much. Police officers are trained to be able to tell when someone's lying and their kids all the more. There's also a network of information that gets around as well, especially in rural areas. If an officer's kid gets into trouble, there's a good chance he'll find out about it.

One tendency for law enforcement parents is the need to protect. We had a situation with our nineteen-year-old daughter in that she and her girlfriends befriended a boy who was very handsome and likable. Because they met him at a church youth group, the assumption was made that he was a great guy, and one of the girls developed a dating relationship with him. Then Brent found out that the boy was going to court for stealing a car and had a prior for marijuana possession. Oh, the tearful conversations we had to have with that one! We talked about boundaries with a person who engages in criminal activity even though likable and that it was a bad idea that he come to our home. She was convinced that he had changed his ways, yet Brent could tell from his excuses that he hadn't yet experienced a turnaround. Out of respect for Brent, our daughter made a choice to distance herself from him in their group and set boundaries like not driving him places. A couple of months later, he abruptly left the group to live on the streets in another state. Hurt that he left without a word, her friends suddenly realized that hanging out with this guy wasn't the smartest idea.

We can trust our husbands to protect our kids. But sometimes it can go too far. I had a conversation recently with an officer who'd seen a lot of death on duty. I asked him how he dealt with it. He told me that it manifested itself in being overprotective of his wife and kids. He has forbid them to go anywhere at times and won't allow people to drive them anywhere unless he first okays it. As you can imagine, this hasn't gone over well. Arguments ensued, and his wife thought he was being jealous. But that's not what it was. It was his inward responses to watching people die in his arms, guarding a little girl's dead body for hours to comfort a friend, and wiping another officer's blood off his uniform. It was these horrible images that manifested themselves into fear for his family.

These situations are so tricky because his fear is valid. The need to control is very real and possibly the only thing he can do to ensure the safety of his loved ones. But it's also problematic. The answer here is to recognize the reasons for the behavior and work from there to communicate. Your officer needs to be validated and respected in the process, and together you can move toward a workable solution.

Outward appearance may be a big deal to a police parent as well. Earrings, tattoos, baggy pants, and hairstyles matter to police officers. I've listened to several of our non-law enforcement friends talk about not making a big deal out of phases their kids go through. But police officers make judgments every shift about people they deal with on the street. Their lives can depend on it. They are looking for signs of criminal behavior and if the individual has a weapon. There are clues they look for in clothing and behavior, and some of these same clues may appeal to our own kids at some point. But law enforcement parents just don't want their kids even remotely resembling the people they put in jail.

Parenting Through Seasons of Childhood

The big picture of parenting is to train children to be grounded, moral, responsible adults. The journey is filled with years of trial and error, learning along the way for both parents and children. The way we parent changes through the stages and seasons of their lives, in purpose and approach.

Early Childhood

This stage is mostly about being present, being playful, and establishing boundaries. It's also an exhausting stage, physically and mentally. Andrea says, "Toddlers require much more patience than felons."

Because your officer works long hours or is on call, the time spent with little ones may not always be as much as they desire. But when they are home, being present means paying attention, even when they're tired. Encourage them to engage, especially when they don't feel like it—it may be just the thing to rejuvenate by activity, laughter and connection.

Brent loves little children—he has a way with them that is so precious. Recently we were talking with a mom in the parking lot whose deputy husband was out of town. They have three very active boys, ages six, three and 18 months. The boys were climbing in and out of the car, honking the horn, and were a little out of control, but Mom desperately needed to talk with me. So, Brent and another guy with us decided to keep the boys occupied for a bit. After about 20 minutes, I look over and see the 18-month-old in Brent's arms, head down and perfectly content. Our eyes met, and I melted at the sight of Brent's smile. It had been a rough couple of months at the department, and I could see the stress fading away, simply by holding a cuddly little one.

Elementary Years to Pre-Teen

This stage is about education and character training. Our kids are involved, exploring new things, and learning about the world they live in through home, school, and their experiences.

Life gets a little more complicated for police families, as the kids now have their own schedule that more often than not conflicts with shift work. This is where creative parenting is crucial. Set the expectation—your officer is not going to make every event. But make the ones he can attend all the more special. We play a special role here. We can use technology to record dance recitals, soccer games, and school plays and then watch with our officers later as a family.

Use time off to your advantage. Enlist kids to wash the car or do yard work together, and then grab an ice cream or a movie. If your officer has to run into the office for a short time, have him take one of the kids and introduce them to the other officers. They will love to see where your officers gets dressed, or how the lights work on the patrol car.

Our friends had a police birthday party for their son, Landon. His mom invited officers to come in uniform, and a retired K-9 did a demonstration. The kids and parents interacted with police on a fun level, building community and trust. After Nerf target practice and toy police car races, they were given junior badge stickers and sent on their way with awesome memories.

Jason and his wife decided that they would choose homeschooling as a way to spend more time with the children. They each take turns teaching in his off-duty time, creating some balance for the kids and much-needed breaks for Mom. Brent and I also chose to homeschool for several years; the kids were able to get that time with him no matter what shift he worked.

Officers can also help with conflict resolution when the kids are in a disagreement. When Gary came home for lunch on duty, his boys had gotten into trouble. Dee was trying to get to the bottom of the conflict but it was frustrating. She asked Gary to step in. Moments later she returned outside to see the kids separated, individually questioned, and he had the truth based on testimony. Mom had to chuckle a bit, as Gary had used his investigative techniques in his parenting. Awesome!

Teenagers

Some people think that teenagers are somewhat of a lost cause. Not true. They are very eager to learn, just in their own way. Teenagers are a lot like toddlers because both stages of life are transitional. Toddlers are transitioning from baby to child. They are very independent, trying new things on their own. They learn to walk, talk, dress themselves, and how to relate with other people—the basics of life as a child.

By comparison, teenagers are transitioning from child to adult. They are very independent, trying new things on their own. They learn who they are, where they fit in, how to dress, and how to relate to all kinds of people—the basics of life as an adult.

It's easy to see how toddlers need their parents to set boundaries to keep them from danger. It's also easy to see that when they don't want your help ("I do it!"), that's just not going to work out. Parents have to step in, despite the pushback of very strong-willed and determined toddlers.

Teenagers are not that different. They, too, need parents to set boundaries to keep them from danger. In fact, I don't have to tell you the danger is even greater. Teenagers still need their parents' help, it's just a little trickier because they talk back, they're not always with you, and are even more independent. But we as parents still have to step in despite the pushback of very strong-willed and determined teens.

One of the ways that was effective to teach our kids some valuable life lessons was through volunteer work. They've learned about life outside of their protective cocoon, saw and felt the suffering of others less fortunate, and had to dig deep when out of their comfort zone.

At least once a year our church youth department puts together a service trip. Our church is located in a wealthy area, so it is a priority that our kids see poverty and get their hands dirty. Brent and my oldest daughter went on a trip to San Francisco to serve meals to homeless people and halfway houses. It was a partnership with an inner city ministry and our church. On this trip, Brent was driving to a location in the Upper Tenderloin with six girls in tow. They turned a corner, and right in front of them was a knife attack happening in the middle of the street. The girls screamed in terror. Brent slipped into cop mode. "QUIET!" he yelled to get their attention. It was instantly silent. In a soft voice, he told the girls that they were to sit tight, make sure all the doors were locked, and then dialed 911. Within a short time, San Francisco PD showed up and took the perp into custody. The girls were fearful and shaken.

After Brent field-ID'd the suspect and provided a statement, there was discussion amongst leadership as to how to deal with the fallout. Some of the other parents wanted to just ignore the incident so that parents at home wouldn't freak out. But Brent saw it as a training opportunity. They pulled all of the teams together, let the girls tell their story, and then Brent explained things from a police perspective. He was able to educate the kids on how crime happens (it was a drug deal gone bad) and the risks drugs bring, and then talk about how to deal with something like this when face to face with it.

Powerful lessons for thirteen- and fourteen-year-old kids.

When Brent and our daughter returned home from the trip, they told me about the knife fight. I was concerned about her seeing something so violent and asked about it. She really wasn't traumatized by it—the debrief alleviated her fear. (Insert commercial here for Critical Incident Stress Debriefs.)

Volunteer work is a great way to talk/serve with your teenagers (or younger). Once they get a taste of this, they've got a new barometer for fun. One of our kids told me that she would rather spend a week playing with impoverished kids in Mexico than party. Interaction, smiles and laughter versus a buzz that hurts in the morning—in her mind, there is no comparison. Volunteer service has been an important key to shaping our kids into who they are today.

One more thing on teenagers. They respond well to mutual trust and respect. Spouses talk about how their officers will interrogate their kids, treating them like criminals. Fear does that. A lack of trust will do that, too.

When we educate our kids about the dangers that lurk nearby and showing we love them through actions and words, we build trust. We take this very seriously in our home—because without trust, relationships can't be healthy. We actually talk about trust, how we've built it over the years, and how a simple bad choice can injure that trust. We give explanations for expectations. Trust hangs in the balance.

Your kids may make stupid choices. A little grace mixed in with consequences goes a long way to influence and guide them through it. Always keep in mind that your goal is to raise a responsible young man or woman, not a perfect one.

Young Adults

Many parents think that the teenage years are the most difficult for a parent. We've learned that the young adult stage is by far the hardest. Why? Because we no longer have control. It's the stage of parenting where we have to trust in the training that we provided for our children over the years, and hope and pray they were listening.

They're making decisions—important ones. On their own. Understanding unfolds as their minds fully develop and life experience takes hold.

In this stage of parenting, we are letting go. Wow, that's a scary thing. Because they're still young, and they're going to make mistakes like we did. The last thing they need is helicopter-parents.

Because Brent and I are in this stage of life with our kids, I'll share three things that are working for us:

- Listen when they want to talk. More often than not it's when we're tired or distracted. It's inconvenient, but crucial. In fact, this is key to building relationship and lasting influence with your adult child.
- Resist the urge to deter consequences of their choices. Natural consequences are amazing teachers.
- Encouragement empowers. Double down on the positive—they need our support. Their future is bright, in spite of and in some cases because of a setback.

Mom and Dad: United Front

So, what if you have a different parenting philosophy than your husband? What if you don't match up on the expectations of your children? Who determines what the rules will be?

Both of you do. If the two of you have different standards of behavior for your kids, nobody wins. Your kids will be confused for a while, and then they'll figure it out and be very smart. They will parent shop and inadvertently pit the two of you against each other. At that point it becomes a real mess. But if you and your husband have different viewpoints, you'll do yourself a huge favor and unify.

Start with things you both want your children to embrace. Morals. Values. Education. Faith. The big things you both want to instill in your children. Then work from there. Look for positive ways to teach them, such as spending time and actually talking about values. When situations arise you can use them as teaching moments. How you conduct yourself in the home and with others is also instilling your values in them as they watch you. Ask yourselves, "Where are the boundaries?" and "What are the consequences of crossing those boundaries?"

Brad and Heidi valued truthfulness in their kids. They felt that if they could trust what their children said, they could build core values on that trust. Because kids are tempted to lie, they came up with a serious consequence: it was Tabasco sauce on the tongue. Fully edible and harmless, it brought temporary pain. It was a powerful deterrent for their children, a lesson that lies cause real pain. They didn't have much trouble with their kids telling the truth after that.

Children need to know where the boundaries are and the consequences of wandering outside those boundaries. Most law enforcement parents understand this because they administer the consequences of those who don't have boundaries every shift. But here's the key: children who have lovingly been given the perimeters for behavior and firm follow up to help them rely on those boundaries feel secure. It doesn't mean they won't try to push the limits. But it gives them peace, knowing that they have room to grow and be kids within the safety of balanced behavior. These perimeters also give the child a sense of dignity.

A couple of years ago, Brent and I had an issue with one of our teenagers. There was a breakdown in trust as boundaries were broken. For the first time, we found ourselves with different views on how to handle things. Brent took an aggressive approach, and I preferred to be more passive, seeing our child's point of view. Both of us loved our child fiercely, but we had differences in how to respond. As the months passed and things began to improve, I realized I had taken sides with my teenager. This wasn't wise. I could see both sides, but because I didn't align myself completely with my husband, I caused more harm to their relationship and ours. Brent didn't feel supported, and I think our child lost some respect for me in the process. But it's never too late; we talked it out and realized there were more similarities than differences that we could agree and act on. The most important thing was to be unified as parents and a couple.

When you and your husband set the boundaries for your kids, respect his instincts. It's always better to set the bar a little higher and adjust later if needed as you both grow in your parenting. Giving more privileges up front and then taking them back later causes a lot of frustration in your kids.

Kid Communication

Kendra's six-year-old son knew Daddy went to work to arrest bad guys. Diedra and her husband sat their boys down at the ages of twelve and ten and had a heart to heart about what Dad's job entailed. Betty's eight- and nine-year-old kids watched their daddy on television during a standoff. I have been asked over and over, what are the guidelines for letting our kids know what their daddy does? How much information is okay and when?

As I've thought about this question, I've realized that there's no formal answer. It really depends on the relationship you have with your kids, what you think they can handle at what age. I don't remember ever sitting our children down to have a heart to heart about Daddy's job. If they had questions, we provided an age-appropriate response. We didn't offer more than what we thought they could handle at the time but made sure we answered their questions truthfully. I don't remember our kids ever fearing for their dad's safety on duty. I think this is because Brent and I never made it a habit to worry about what could happen, and they took their cues from us.

I do know that our kids suffered disappointment when Brent wasn't there for sports games, Fourth of July fireworks, and other things that came up here and there. Over the years he's tried to make as many events as he can, but there were times he just couldn't be there. But if there was something important that he couldn't make it to, we always tried to make up for it later.

When Brent was commuting to the Bay Area during the week and home on weekends only, he had to miss many kid events. Our youngest daughter was in a program through our church in which she conquered challenges weekly and received promotions in return, using a medieval theme as the backdrop. They had really great ceremonies where the child would be honored for their accomplishment. But the ceremony was on a Wednesday night. She was really sad that Dad was gone. We told her that although he wouldn't be able to be there, we would tape it so he could see it later. What we didn't tell her was that Brent worked out his schedule and drove back that night, arriving just in time. The look on her face when she saw him was priceless. She burst into big, happy tears and ran to hug him really tightly.

With a little planning and creativity, we can redeem the events our husbands miss. As moms, we have to lower the expectations of our kids when the career calls. But when we take the time to make special efforts to make memories, it makes up for it. In fact, these are some of the best days of their lives.

Communication in a Post-Ferguson World

When our children are school age and teenagers, they will hear anti-police rhetoric at school or even among their friends. As I drove several high school football players to a game, we drove up next to a motor officer at a stoplight. Germaine, one of our favorites of our son's friends said, "Eww. The PoPo." Another kid says, "Dude—you know what David's dad does, right?" He responded, "Oh, yeah. Your dad's a cop! I didn't think about that." We were able to gently and humorously point the fact out that cops are people, too, and they are there to protect us.

When our young ones hear stuff at school, they may not be as confident, or have trust built up with those who are talking trash. It's a good idea to check in from time to time to make sure they're not being bullied for their parent being a cop. It may also help to have Dad or Mom come to the school in uniform and be accessible and human. If your child hears stuff, address it with truth, replacing fear and confusion with truth and encouragement.

Gun Safety

When our oldest son was little, we got a kick out the way he tied his cuddle blanket around his neck, made guns out of whatever was around, and ran off to fight the bad guys. When Brent's leather holders for badges and guns were retired, our son appointed himself heir to them. Then as he got older, it was Nerf guns and laser tag. At times our home was converted into a war zone, with the screens taken out of the windows, the lights out, and sweaty boys hiding, shooting foam darts at each other, and leaping in and out of the house through the windows—*serious* fun. He progressed to Air Soft guns and paintball as a teenager. He and his buddies found empty fields with lots of bushes, trees, and ditches and got down and dirty, strategizing all the way. I think he even borrowed some of Brent's old Kevlar panels and eye gear to protect himself from welts.

As you can see, we have a relaxed view of guns in our family. But that doesn't mean we don't take gun safety seriously. When Brent brings his duty weapon home, he keeps it secure and teaches the kids about how the gun works and the correct way to handle it. He also cleans his weapon at work. There is an attitude of respect, not making a big deal out of it, but rather stressing the importance of keeping it pointed away from everyone even when it is unable to fire. The kids know that they are never to handle it by themselves and under no circumstances with another child. This would never happen anyway; Brent keeps his gun with him and will leave it in his locker at work more often than not.

If your home has other weapons, though, it is imperative that you get a safe that is childproof. We all know of a tragic story or two where accidents have happened. Kids can be unpredictable even when we train them. Talk with your kids about guns at friends' homes as well or if someone brings a weapon to school. They may respect your rules at home, but their curiosity may get the best of them somewhere else. We also use news of gun accidents to remind them of what to do in these situations.

Guns aren't the only law enforcement equipment we need to think about. Kids also need to understand that they don't want to get into the pepper spray, Taser, or the handcuffs. One afternoon Brent laid his gun belt on the bed right beside me, and our youngest son asked to see the handcuffs. Brent got them out and gave them to him. But before we could say anything, he put them on himself and started laughing. Until he realized that Brent's handcuff keys were at the office, forty minutes away! It took some rummaging through the junk drawers and a call to a cop neighbor before we finally found an extra key. Our son doesn't go near the handcuffs anymore. Sometimes natural consequences cure whatever foolishness our kids dish up.

Dads Need Their Kids

When Brent became a highway patrolman, I was the one who comforted him when he came home. But after we started having children, I noticed a little shift. It seemed to me that he was more excited to see them than me when he came home. I used to get a little jealous, but then realized why he did this.

I've come to understand that my husband needs and feeds off of his kids. He needs their optimism. He needs their innocence and affection. He sees in them that there is good in the world, and it's worth fighting for. I know that may sound a little dramatic, but it's true. He may not even realize it. But coming home and holding his baby girl or wrestling on the floor with his boys—my husband needed this. Chances are so does yours.

Almost every day, year after year, there was a wrestling session at our home. It started when our oldest daughter could crawl. Brent tackled her—lovingly, of course—and she would laugh until her belly hurt. It continued through the years, and as they grew we had to clear a large space, as the legs and arms were much longer, but the laughter still rang through the halls. I called it wrestle therapy, and Brent needed it just as much as the kids.

But I've always been the stick in the mud. I was the one who moved the vase or scolded when it got too rough. And they laughed at me and sometimes pulled me in against my will. Usually it ended with my stomach aching because I couldn't stop laughing. We miss those days now, although sometimes my son will tackle me onto something soft and then Brent comes to my rescue. I'm protesting the whole time, but you know I absolutely love it.

So, let them wrestle. Let them throw footballs (soft ones) in at least one room of the house. Let them cuddle past bedtime. It is good for our husbands' souls, and it helps to balance out the harder parts of his job. The kids love it. And you probably will, too.

On the Other Hand...

There are other seasons in a law enforcement career that aren't so great for kids. Sometimes your husband will need some quiet, alone time. When he's had a really bad day, he might not be able to handle the chaos that kids create. Several of my law enforcement friends have told me that they have had to take the kids somewhere else or send their husbands to the gym. Being quick to anger, irritable, or just in his own little world is a reality at some point. Unfortunately this can be really hurtful to the children who don't understand.

That's where we come in. Our husbands need a little space, exercise, time, or sleep to get back on track. We can create room for this, depending on our creativity and our attitudes. If we're full of resentment, our kids will pick up on it and be resentful. If we are patient, our kids will try to be patient. If we give him a little room for moods, it won't be so traumatic for the kids. Then, when he's calmed down a bit, you and the kids can engage him in the family goings on.

It's important to communicate to your kids, no matter what the age, what is going on. For little ones you can tell them that Daddy's had a bad day, and he needs some time to deal with it. For older kids you can give a little more detail, as appropriate. But the attitude is support and love, not condemnation. We all have moods from time to time, and home is the best place to work through them, especially if we give each other the space to do it.

A CHiP Off the Ol' Block

I felt like I'd just been socked in the gut. I had the phone in my ear, and my son had just announced he needed his birth certificate ASAP, as he was joining the Marines. Oof. It came out of left field and reduced me to tears.

Now, you have to understand something. I'd been a law enforcement wife for over twenty years. I'd dealt with the risks and realities of what that means. But it's different when it's your baby.

My friend Brenna agrees wholeheartedly. Things were vastly different when her sons joined the highway patrol as opposed to her husband. "My husband was a man, but I still look at my boys as my children. It's very different with your kids. I'm proud of them. I think it's a great career, but it's hard to see them out there on the road."

So, what's a mom to do when her babies grow up and follow in their Dad's footsteps?

As I've interviewed several of my friends who are in this situation, I've come up with a few ideas. Ideas that I will be using if any of my kids choose police work.

- If it's fear you're feeling, **deal with it head on**. Go back to chapter five and reread with your kids in mind.
- **Bond with other law enforcement parents**. It's always better to trek the journey with others who get it.
- **Let go**. If your child is going into this line of work, he/she's an adult. If you're struggling and you have a close relationship, maybe you could line up some phone calls to get you acclimated. Brenna did this. She had her son call her when he got home after every shift for the first couple months. He was willing to do this for her, and she eventually made peace within herself. She let go, and he's doing well.
- **Be there for your child's spouse**. Remember that this is all new to them, and you could be a great resource for talking things through. Make yourself available, but don't interfere.
- **Enjoy the interaction** between your officer and your child. There will be a new bond there that is enjoyable to watch. It's satisfying to see your child grow up and follow in the family way. Support, love, and enjoy.

The Greatest Gift

Finally, the best way to support your kids and your family as a unit is to build a good marriage. Your kids thrive when you and your husband are working together, giving each other support through good times and bad. They are learning the positive value of loving in all circumstances. It doesn't have to be perfect. Just real.

—∞∞∞—

Discussion Group Questions

1. Are you a daughter of a police officer? If so, describe your memories and how they affected you.
2. Talk about some ways to create memories with children and Officer amidst his schedule.
3. Talk about how your husband needs his kids. Do you agree with this? Have you noticed this in your own family?
4. Put together a law enforcement group event that is especially for the kids. Your officers may have some great ideas to incorporate awareness, cool law enforcement stuff, K-9s, and other educational and relational activities.

CHAPTER 13

TO SERVE AND PROTECT (YOUR MARRIAGE, THAT IS!)

*In addition to strength and courage from my
wife, I also received grace, beauty, patience,
forgiveness, and the one person who loves
me more than anyone else on this earth.*

MICHAEL, TEXAS

Marriage is an armed alliance against the outside world.

GILBERT KEITH CHESTERSON

*Being a good husband is like being a gardener.
You've got to give your partner lots of water
and sunshine (love and support).*

JACK BLACK

In October 2010, the Pew Research Center came out with a survey that claimed four out of ten American adults feel that marriage is becoming obsolete.[22] That's alarming, considering that marriage/family is the foundational unit for society as a whole. There are many assaults on marriages these days—outside pressures, inward hurts, past baggage, other relationships (in-laws, exes, adultery), and an overall lack of marital know how. They threaten the overall well being of two people who have committed their lives to one another as well as the children involved.

But our marriages are worth fighting for.

---

22 http://today.msnbc.msn.com/id/40239472/ns/today-today_health/from/toolbar

Just like our husbands take an oath to serve and protect the public from lawlessness and to preserve the peace no matter the cost, we can choose to serve and protect our marriages as well. The following is an adaptation from a Texas police officer's oath that I found online.[23] What if we each took an oath that looks like this:

As a partner in this marriage, my fundamental duty is to serve my spouse; to safeguard our union; to protect our commitment against those who would seek to destroy it, and to respect the person to whom I'm bound in liberty, equality, and love.

I will keep myself unsullied as an example to my children; maintain courageous calm in the face of conflict and difficult circumstances; develop self-restraint; and be constantly mindful of the welfare of my family. Honest in thought and deed within my marriage, I will be exemplary in keeping myself only to my spouse. Whatever I see or hear in a confidential nature or that my spouse confides in me will be kept ever secret unless given permission to share with others.

I will never act unbecomingly or permit feelings of animosity and unforgiveness to influence my decisions in this marriage. With no compromise and relentless tenacity, I will devote myself to my spouse courteously and appropriately without fear, malice or ill will, never employing unnecessary force or violence.

I recognize the ring on my finger as a symbol of commitment, and I accept it as a sacred trust to be held so long as I live. I will constantly strive to achieve these objectives and ideals, dedicating myself before God to my chosen partner… my spouse.

As cop wives, we have committed ourselves to lay down certain rights of ours for the greater good of our country, state, county, or city. It takes courage, determination, and unselfishness to see this through. Likewise, we must pledge to do the same with each other, to ensure our marriages are healthy and thriving for the duration of our lives together. And it doesn't require anything less than the same attitudes mentioned above.

---

23 http://answers.yahoo.com/question/index?qid=20080424104517AAJvlFj

We must serve and protect our marriages much like officers serve and protect the population.

Serve Your Marriage Well: Build Trust

To have a thriving relationship we must have trust. Trust is a "firm belief or confidence in the honesty, integrity, reliability, justice, etc. of another person or thing."[24] When Brent and I started dating each other, we had guarded trust. We didn't know each other yet. Then over time that confidence grew through experience as we learned more about each other's character. At some point, you and I made commitments and pledged vows at our weddings to honor those commitments. These were formal declarations of trust in each other, our firm belief that our spouses will follow through on their word.

One of the main reasons I chose Brent to share my life with is that I saw that he had integrity. He was loyal and did what he said he would do. This was incredibly important to me because in my dating experience this was very hard to find. Relationship after relationship ended because of another girl entering the picture; they simply found someone they wanted more. This left me with a couple of problems. First, the hurt ran deep. It surfaced in unattractive ways like jealousy and suspicion. Second, I didn't trust men. But Brent was very different from the other guys I had dated. He seemed trustworthy, so I decided to take a chance one last time.

I wish I could say it was easy to build trust in Brent. But it wasn't. Not because of anything he did or didn't do but because inwardly I was programmed to expect he would, at some point, leave me for someone else. It was my feeble protection from getting hurt. But, in spite of my trust issues, he has been faithful to me for almost thirty years now. Building trust, or confidence, in his character and our relationship has been a slow but sure process as we navigate through life together. I have put him through a lot, but he's been very patient with me, reassuring me and loving me in the midst of my shortcomings. It's been a tough but beautiful transformation as we build trust together.

---

24 Webster's New World College Dictionary

Deposits into the Trust Account

Building trust in your relationship takes a lifetime. As the years progress, there will be deposits and withdrawals as we rise and fall to each other's expectations. I mentioned this in chapter six. Much like a bank account, we give and take from our relationships. Here are some ways to invest in our marriages.

Time Is Not a Luxury

We need to spend time together alone. This is a no brainer, right? Perhaps when relationships are young the thought of not spending time together is ludicrous. But when kids are added to the mix, careers take more time than usual, and responsibilities pile up; believe me, spending time together can seem like a luxury. But it isn't a luxury. It's a need, and as all these other things crowd our lives, we need time together all the more. This is when we have to get creative and *intentional*.

We need this time to get in sync with one another. As we grow older, we undergo changes good and difficult. We need to dream together about the future no matter how long we've been married. We need to talk about things we enjoy individually and together. We need to laugh together. We need to set financial goals. We need to share a vision for our kids. All of this requires time to talk through. Whether we've been married three years or thirty, these conversations are crucial to us as individuals and as couples.

Four Levels of Communication

We must learn to explore all four levels of communication that we employ. The first is housekeeping. This is the everyday talking of who's picking up the kids or "I'll be working an overtime detail this Friday." The second level is sharing what happened in the course of the day while we're apart. For police officers this may require a different level of trust in the spouse than non-law enforcement because of the potential gravity of what has actually happened in his day. Building trust at this level means that the response be appropriate. If an officer shares with his spouse that he watched a man die on duty, her ability to handle that information actually increases or decreases his trust in her. Because of this the third level may be intimately related. The third level is when we share parts of ourselves, responses to the goings on of the day. Hopes and fears come out at this level and, depending on each others' responses, lay the groundwork for the deep conversations.

Mike and Trina have been married thirty-two years, and he is newly retired from law enforcement. When Trina recently brought home an issue she was really bothered about, Mike quickly came up with a solution. This wasn't the response Trina was looking for. Instantly there was conflict. She wasn't coming to him with a problem that needed solving but rather for him to be quiet and let her process it through. As an officer Mike was there to fix the problem. At home he needed a different, more delicate approach.

The last level of communication springs from an appropriate, trusted response to level three. As Mike listens to Trina, asking clarifying questions and being patient while she processes it through, something incredible happens. Intimacy. There is a soul-to-soul connection that says, "I'm safe. You can trust me with your vulnerabilities." When we learn to respond to each other out of love, the protective layers of self-preservation come off, and we can share pieces of who we are without fear. We can communicate on a soul-to-soul level.

As we move through the four levels of communication, we build trust in each other as we engage. As you make deposits of time and choose to listen in a way that feels safe to your partner, you can get to that soul-to-soul level.

Keep Your Word

We need to keep our word. Believe it or not, sometimes this can be difficult for law enforcement marriages. Not that we lie, for we generally place great value on truth. It's more than this. It's about follow through. Life in law enforcement can be one unkept promise after another. With a crisis-driven career and a sincere love for it, sometimes an officer can't (or won't) always live up to what he promises. Many officers' wives harden because too many promises go unmet and wound her. After awhile she will develop protections against getting hurt again, and that will show up as frustration, sarcasm, and disrespect. She doesn't trust anymore.

This is not just about cops. It's universal. If you promise to call your mother, call your mother. If you say you'll pay the water bill, pay it on time. If you resolve to go on a vacation for the first time in two years, make choices that will allow it to happen. Focused follow up is crucial to build trust.

Build Each Other Up

Fourth, build each other up. We all need encouragement, some more than others. As we grow closer to our spouses, we will learn the most effective ways of building each other up and, unfortunately, tearing down. With some, encouragement comes through words. With others, it's respect. Still others, it's cooking a good meal.

Nothing makes us unsafe more than when we tear down other people with our actions and words. Your comfort level of straight talk will depend upon the way your own family communicated with each other. If you come from a family of cops, chances are you can take it head on. If you come from a more sensitive family, you may get hurt easily. My family was the type to just let it go and not talk about the hard stuff. It took me a long time to be able to communicate delicate issues without feeling attacked or that I was wounding someone else. When Brent gave me permission to express my frustration with him verbally, we built trust.

Get Real

Be real. I read an interview with actor Jack Black in which he talks about marriage. "I have a tendency to do whatever my wife wants," he confides, "and then anger builds up inside me and comes out in little passive-aggressive bursts. It's better to just communicate your desires up front from the get-go."[25] How many times do we play this game? Either we don't know how we feel about things, or we just don't want to deal with

25 http://www.parade.com/celebrity/celebrity-parade/2010/1205-jack-black-gullivers-travels.html

the issue at hand. Instead, we don't communicate and then let drama develop.

Brianna felt this way about her husband, Mark, when he was working a lot of hours on the road. "I was just too demanding. I wanted him home. I would get upset," she admits, "I would never really come out and say that, but it came out in other ways. Cold shoulder, rude. I would be upset, and he wouldn't even know why."

We are so good at this! I used to put Brent through this all the time. He had to work to get my true feelings out of me. It was a little game I played, and, boy, did it get old after a couple of years. I'm glad to say that I have learned to be real the first time. I am only able to do this because my husband and I have built up trust over the years.

Lastly, nurture intimacy. Oh, yes, we have to go *there*. Sex, the ultimate intimate act, definitely builds trust. And if there are issues with sex, it can tear trust apart.

A Few Words about Sex...

Every time I get women together to talk about marriage, inevitably the conversation will veer toward sex. In fact, when I had a group of newly-wed wives over to talk about several aspects of marriage, I couldn't get them to talk about anything else! For hours we delved into the subject of marital sex amidst giggles and tears. There are always questions, there are always hurts, and there is always some confusion.

I know of four marriages just off the top of my head in which the wife stopped having sex with her husband. Three ended in divorce, and the jury is still out on the third (not looking good). If you are married and healthy but are not having sex regularly, there is an underlying problem that needs to be addressed.

Sex is a beautiful experience that creates intimacy within committed love. It literally brings two people together and makes them one. There is no other act that is as binding, no other act that is as pleasurable, and no other act that is so vulnerable. When we have sex, we are inviting our spouse into our most private places, giving and taking of ourselves in an incredibly intimate way. At that point there is nothing between us. Healthy sex between a married couple builds trust.

So why are so many couples struggling in this area? Why are husbands and wives withholding themselves from each other? And why does it seem like we don't want to have sex after we're married when we couldn't keep our hands off each other before? I'm not an expert, but based on many conversations over the years, I've come up with five circumstances that affect our sexual relationships as law enforcement couples.

The first circumstance relates to our husbands' schedules. Shift work can be really difficult on the frequency of sex. Mandy and George both worked for government agencies. She worked the day shift in an office, and he worked graveyards in the jail. For the first three years of their marriage, they literally passed each other on the freeway coming and going to work. They rarely shared a bed together. However, they got creative and made it work, even becoming pregnant during that time!

The second circumstance has to do with the seasons we go through over the years. As newlyweds, we are adventurous and eager, but then when small children start filling the home, the quantity of sex tends to wane. Young moms have so many demands—little ones hanging on them and needing constant attention. They are always tired. It's hard to feel sexy when Mom is sporting extra baby weight and wearing dirty T-shirts all the time. When Marlo suggests a little tryst in the bedroom in the middle of the day, Erica tries to comply. But she says, "Shifting from diapers to sex is difficult for me. I'm willing to take one for the team, but I need more time to enjoy this!"

As kids grow older, there seems to be a little more desire for sex. Susan and her husband, Jason, have three school-age boys. When a few of us brought up the fact that it's hard to find the time to have sex, her response was, "It doesn't take long, people! Sometimes we just head for the laundry room and lock ourselves in for a quickie!" After young adult kids leave the house, I've heard several friends comment that they feel like newlyweds again, having sex wherever and whenever, just because they can!

The third circumstance is stress. When we deal with heavy stuff and our lives become difficult, sex seems to take a back seat. However, this is when we may have to be proactive, choosing to have sex together. Nancy calls this "mercy sex." She understands that her husband, Tom, needs to have sex frequently. She doesn't need it as often, and it requires some sacrifice on her part, especially when she's had a stressful day at work or with her three boys. But she willingly and cheerfully engages in mercy sex with her husband out of love for him. In stressful times the desires may not be there because we're distracted, but when we make the effort to please each other, it seems to relieve some of that pent up tension. And it builds trust.

Perhaps we're not the ones who are the stressed out ones. Perhaps your officer is the one who doesn't seem as interested as he used to be. Sandra and Dave's sex life was waning. The kids were older as were they, but Sandra's libido was calling! Dave would fall asleep early or stay up late. It seemed to Sandra that he was avoiding her. It became an issue for the first time in their life together. After awhile, they realized it was the stress Dave was under at work. He had some unbelievable demands on him for many months, and the last thing on his mind was sex. They decided to make a date every weekend—a compromise. It worked. The expectation was there, and they made it work for the duration of the stress. Frequency returned once the stress subsided.

The last two circumstances are a little more difficult to overcome. The first is past baggage. It is possible that one of you may have suffered pain because of sex. Abuse, molestation, or past relationships that bring painful memories back may be the reason for disinterest in sex. Sex between a married couple is an amazing thing, but if sex is a negative in your mind because of a painful experience, you may not be able to get there. In her book *Kiss Me Again – Restoring Lost Intimacy in Marriage* Barbara Wilson says,

> *Rape or abuse is a big deal. If this is your story, please understand it wasn't your fault. Even so, you will not "get over it" on your own. Until you have healing, sex with your husband will continue to trigger negative emotions, including shame, that will prevent you from being able to trust him and be vulnerable with him emotionally and physically. The lack of trust and emotional intimacy will diminish your enjoyment of and desire for sex.*[26]

---

26 Barbara Wilson, *Kiss Me Again*, (Colorado Springs, CO: Multnomah Books, 2009) page 22.

If this is the case for you, you need healing. Talk together about this; many times a couple can work through it with the help of a counselor. I know several women who have suffered rape and child abuse. After their journeys of healing, they found hope as their emotional and sexual relationships with their husbands improved.

The last circumstance is one you may not have heard of. It's sexual bonding from past relationships. The idea is that each time you have sex with a partner, you bond with that person physically, emotionally, and physiologically. I again refer to Barbara Wilson:

> *Scientists have discovered that in addition to releasing chemicals [endorphins and enkephalins] during sex, the brain also releases a hormone called oxytocin, and these work together to create a strong bond between people. This invisible bond works like superglue, permanently attaching us emotionally and spiritually to a lover. This bonding happens with everyone with whom we have sex—whether we're married or single, and whether the sex is consensual or forced. The past ten years have produced cutting-edge research on this hormone, which scientists have dubbed the hormone of love.*[27]

This powerful hormone of love is designed to keep us bonded for a lifetime. But if we have had past sexual relationships, this also happened with each person we had sex with. Can you see how this could be an issue? If we have been bonded with someone sexually, break away from them, then repeat the process again (and again), this can leave us broken and racked with emotional pain. Another problem is this hormone of love decreases with each partner. This explains why some people can have casual, non-committed sex with multiple partners. If you or your husband are experiencing a lack of desire, it could be that you have bonded with other people intimately, and it's affecting the sexual relationship you now have with your spouse.

There is hope here though. You can break these bonds and get healing. But it's a process that requires much more explanation. If this is

27 Barbara Wilson, *Kiss Me Again*, (Colorado Springs, CO: Multnomah Books, 2009) page 28-29.

something that rings familiar, you may want to pick up the book I referred to earlier.

Withdrawals from the Trust Account

When we are building trust in our marriages, unfortunately there will be some things that will cause us to mistrust. None of us married a perfect person; perfect people only exist in fairy tales. Inevitably we will let each other down. Expecting this from the get-go, we may be able to let things slide here and there, but there are things we do that negatively affect trust.

The first is **comparisons**. Even though we are married, most of us lead different lives while we are apart. Because officers are dealing with life and death, we can make assumptions that he will have the tougher job. But that doesn't mean that taking care of the kids at home isn't stressful too. Or working at the bank. Or volunteering at the community center. However we spend our time, there will be stress as well.

Melissa is new to this whole journey. Her husband has been a patrolman for only two years, but was a Marine before that. She shared that her biggest struggle is when she has an issue, her husband minimizes it. "He says, 'What's the big deal? Get over it! So she said this and that! Who cares?' He thinks my world is so small and insignificant. But I'm like, 'It's my world. I listen to all of your crap on duty, why can't you just listen to my world? Can't you just *pretend* to care?'"

Ellen chimed in with, "My husband does this too. He says, 'Ooh, catastrophe! Both the PTA drama *and* this other conflict? Oh my gosh!' I know that in the overall scheme of things, I will never out trump him. But it's important to me. So I just call my friend because she cares. And she'll remind me how much I love him. She says, 'I know he's crazy, but he loves you!'"

Comparing ourselves to our officers separates. Perhaps in wanting understanding from one another, we inadvertently alienate the other spouse. Someone comes away devalued because the comparison ends in a place where someone has it better (or worse). More often than not, someone comes away with the feeling that their issue doesn't matter because it's not as bad as their spouse's issue. In Ellen's case it shuts down communication altogether, leaving some doubt in her mind that her husband loves her.

The second withdrawal from the trust account is **trying to control each other**. This is very common in law enforcement marriages. Usually the person who is trying to control the other doesn't mean to hurt anyone. It tends to be a reflection of selfishness and/or fear. Fear of the what-if. Fear of my inability to handle whatever the situation is. Fear of trusting. Yes, I said that right. When we try to control another human being, we are, in essence, saying that we don't trust them. *I need to take control because you are inadequate.* Ouch. Selfishness comes in when we assume that we have to take control because we feel we are superior in our ability: *I'm better equipped than you.* Manipulation can be a result of this as well. *I want something, and I don't trust you enough to just ask for it. I need to get it by fooling you or wearing you down by making you angry.* Do you understand how this can break down trust?

The third withdrawal is the most obvious: **lying**. When we intentionally lead others to believe something other than what is the truth, we lie. There are big lies and small lies in regards to the impact that the lie will have. But they are still lies, and they break down trust.

Most of us lie because we have fallen short in some way and we are too embarrassed to own up to it. We are protecting our pride. Some of us lie to keep from getting caught in something we've done wrong. We are protecting our deceit. Some of us lie because we just don't like the truth.

The last withdrawal is the big one: having an **extramarital affair**. This is the ultimate breech of trust in a marriage and more often than not will break the marriage apart. Someone brings another person into your union, and that person obviously isn't welcome by the spouse. Unfortunately, this happens way too often, but we can safeguard our marriages against it. We just have to set some boundaries.

Protect Your Marriage: Set Boundaries

In the last chapter I talked about boundaries for our kids. I mentioned that these boundaries keep them safe, secure, and they protect their dignity. It is the same for us in our marriage. We too need boundaries to keep our marriage safe, secure, and to protect our dignity as a couple.

Donna has a philosophy about boundaries. She is a very self-assured woman and has survived her husband's twenty-nine-year career in law enforcement intact and with strong beliefs. When I asked her to share with me something that helped her in her marriage, she told me that they set boundaries. It was what helped her maneuver through both of their careers, children, household, etc. She said they first established boundaries. Then they learned to communicate those boundaries. And finally they enforced the boundaries. In Donna's case, she was very aware of what she could and couldn't handle. So she divvyed up responsibilities for the household and then kept everyone accountable. Chores, communication, events, behavior—the expectations were communicated and, for the most part, adhered to.

As our marriages progress in trust and communication, we will learn what each other can handle and what will become an issue. This applies to all aspects of our lives—children, work, family interaction, etc., and thus there will be boundaries that will be made by accident. Boundaries made by accident are usually touchy subjects that we don't want to talk about because they invoke emotion. Some examples are "We never lean against Dad's car," or "We never talk about overeating in our family." But as we intentionally put in perimeters to safeguard our marriages, we need to actually talk about establishing them and why, communicating about them freely, and thus enforcing them in our lives.

The boundaries that we need to instill in our marriages intentionally are those that protect three areas of vulnerability: our minds and emotions, our bodies, and our unions.

Guard Your Mind/Emotions

Actions come from choices. Choices come from mindsets. Therefore we have to start with our minds. Our minds are the key to keeping our emotions in check.

Most extramarital affairs begin with some kind of emotional attraction. This is especially the case for women. Emotional affairs can and do lead to sexual affairs. It usually starts out innocent. There's a mutual respect that leads to more time together. The respect can lead to trust, and, if not checked, vulnerability and dependence develops. This is an emotional affair. We begin to depend on someone other than our spouse for emotional support, and this is dangerous.

This type of thing happened in the aftermath of 9/11. Because so many policemen and firemen were lost, those who survived decided that they would take care of the surviving families. In many cases emotional affairs began as the widows depended emotionally upon these men. The emotional affairs developed into sexual relationships, and some of these men divorced their wives and married the widows. It was devastating on many levels, as wives and children of surviving rescuers eventually lost them to the widows of those who had died. They too became victims of 9/11.

So how do we protect ourselves from emotional affairs? First of all awareness helps. Beware the person who claims that you are the only one who they can talk to. This is a red flag because it isn't true. What is true is that this person has chosen you as their confidant and is already emotionally attached. Run—don't walk—to the nearest exit!

Create boundaries with others in this regard. Learn to keep an eye out for those who would seek to attach themselves emotionally to you. Brent refers to his "Spidey-sense," a feeling that something isn't quite right that puts his guard up even if he can't identify it at a conscious level.

If you find yourself attracted to someone else and really enjoy a connection on an emotional level, distance yourself immediately. Then go the extra mile. Talk about it with a close friend. I have found that any danger lurking in the shadows will disappear when the light is turned on. I have sought accountability from a few close friends who know my husband and love him. I gave them permission to look me in the eye and ask me about attractions. It keeps me accountable.

One last thing. If your emotional needs are being met by your spouse, the temptation to connect with another man is decreased.

Guard Your Body

Every affair begins with a choice to entertain temptations. Our bodies have strong biological needs. Somehow those needs have to be met. So the first way to safeguard yourself from extramarital affairs is to have frequent sex together. Like I said earlier, sometimes this will take an act of the will, depending on circumstances. But if you are investing in a healthy sex life together, temptations toward someone else will naturally decrease.

But what if one of you is in a season of dryness in this area? What if you aren't getting along like you used to? What if our eyes wander toward someone who is attractive? How can we abstain from these temptations when there are problems at home?

We have to be all the more intentional. All the more vigilant. Recognize the enemies that want to destroy our marriage, and be wise to our own vulnerabilities.

Many years ago I went on a trip with my husband. We attended a retirement dinner and then met with some friends at a little club nearby. As we visited, another man joined us. Everyone knew him but me, but I noticed he was very handsome. After we'd been there for awhile, the band started playing these great, older songs. The man started dancing with other ladies at the table and then asked me. Brent, who hates to dance, told me to go ahead. So I did. I danced with this man for several songs, returned to my husband, and that was that. Until he kept creeping into my thoughts.

As I talked this out with a girlfriend, she told me that I needed to watch myself with the dancing. She was right. I realized that dancing was a temptation trigger for me. I resolved to only dance with my husband from then on. We need to understand what turns us on and then reserve that trigger for our spouse. I later shared this with Brent, and, turns out, he is trying to develop a like for dancing because he loves me! We recently took Tango lessons with some friends (his idea), and had a blast!

Another way to safeguard ourselves from adultery is to keep away from the wrong places and the wrong people. I call these danger zones. If someone is coming on to you, cut off contact with them. If your friends are getting wild in Las Vegas, volunteer to be the designated driver or the one who makes sure they don't regret something in the morning. You'll thank yourself later on.

If you are attracted to someone else, make yourself accountable to someone you trust. And that could include your own spouse.

Guard Your Union

I once heard a speaker refer to sex as fire. He said, "A fire in the fireplace will warm a home. Fire outside of the fireplace will burn the house down." In other words, sex has great rewards if it has boundaries. Sex without boundaries can ruin everything. What do I mean by this?

I'm not talking about squashing your creativity in the bedroom. Sex is an intimate, trust-building uniting of two bodies, hearts, and souls. The boundary here is that we keep it just between the two of us. We have to safeguard our union by not letting anything or anyone join us in the bedroom or come between us during sex. This includes other people. This includes pornography. This includes letting our minds wander during sex. Any inclusion of others into our sexual relationship will break down the uniting factor in our relationship. And it will introduce mistrust.

The Perfect Storm

I have a friend I've known for almost 40 years. Recently Jill shared with me that she had an affair. After she peeled me off the floor from the shock (she was the last person I thought would do this), I asked her how it happened.

"It was the perfect storm," she said, "Kevin and I haven't been getting along. Our business was about to go under, we were arguing, we caught our boys smoking pot in the backyard... it seemed like everything in our lives was going wrong. At the same time, I found an old school acquaintance on Facebook. We were talking online, then started meeting together. He was the one thing in my life that brought happiness. We ended up in bed together."

At that point her life went from bad to worse. Their business went bankrupt, everyone was angry and hurt, and this didn't help their boys any. But she admitted it to her husband and took the consequences humbly. She didn't make excuses and apologized to several layers of family. It was touch and go for several months.

With the help of her family and close friends, she and her husband are rebuilding their marriage. They are slowly but surely retraining themselves to do things the right way. Rebuilding trust. Communicating. Choosing attitudes that build up instead of tear down. She is now accountable to friends and doesn't communicate on Facebook with old boyfriends anymore. Even after a serious breech of trust, Jill and Kevin have forgiven each other and are starting over. That takes character. That takes commitment.

What Do I Do if He Has an Affair?

We can try to do what we can to serve and protect our marriages, but sometimes things just go wrong. Infidelity happens, and tears at the very foundations of trust.

There are some cases in which the cop not only has an affair, but chooses to leave his family altogether. If this is your situation, my heart goes out to you. Your choice has been made for you, and you are left in shambles. I hope that you will seek healing in a safe place, with people who love you. At times like this, your support system will carry you forward while you grieve and rebuild.

There are other cases in which the affair happens, but the couple chooses to remain married. In most cases, there were problems before the affair occurred, and this is the event that wakes everybody up. They are devastated, but they choose to work through the grief together and make the changes necessary for a renewed marriage.

I have several girlfriends who have been victims of unfaithfulness; lots of them are married to police officers. Handsome husbands, nice guys, but they got caught up in waywardness. In talking with these gals over the years, I've made some observations that may be helpful should you find yourself in this predicament.

First, most stayed with their husbands after the affair. I asked why. All said the same thing: their husbands were repentant. When they were caught, the husbands felt relief. They wanted their marriages back, and were willing not only to apologize, but to take the time necessary to prove their renewed love. This was the key.

All took the chance to confront their husbands and communicate their hurt. This is very important for healing. When there is a hurt like this, it is imperative that the offending spouse understand that what they've done has damaged their partner, and their marriage. In several cases, there was also a confrontation via phone with the other woman. This seemed to help—it was a kind of reinsertion of their rightful place in their marriage. It also helped them to believe that the affair was indeed over. In one case, my friend didn't want to go there.

All of these women made a choice. They allowed themselves to grieve for a time, but then they chose to forgive. Forgiveness doesn't excuse the behavior, nor assert that what they did was okay. David Stoop, in his book *Forgiving the Unforgivable*, says that "Forgiving other people does not in any way benefit or let them off the hook. It allows us to cancel the debt they owe us, which in all probability they can never pay anyway. We are the ones who are freed—from the expectation of restitution for the wrongs done to us."[28] I admire these ladies. It takes a lot of courage and character to choose to forgive.

Another observation is they surrounded themselves with those who supported their marriage. Trusted family, counselors, clergy, accountability partners, and close friends were crucial to the reconciliation process. These people loved them through the hurt, listened to their cries, and spoke truth into their marriages.

The last thing that all of these gals did was go through the journey to rebuild trust. It wasn't easy, and it wasn't quick. In fact, they're still rebuilding. Their journeys have been two steps forward, one step back, again and again. But all four are on their way back to a better marriage than they had before.

Gratitude Goes a Long Way

The last thing that can protect your marriage is gratitude. When years run together and your marriage seems to take more work, it is easy to begin to lose perspective. We get tired. We are grumpy. And we can concentrate on each other's negative qualities and even be tempted to look elsewhere. Choosing to be grateful for each other can turn this around. We all have weaknesses and things in our character that could use improvement. But that's only half of the story. We all have good qualities, too. When we

28 David Stoop, Forgiving the Unforgivable, (Ventura, CA: Regal Books, 2005) page 34.

choose an attitude of thankfulness for positive things in our spouse, we reinstate value to each other and our relationships. Gratitude protects.

—⊶⊷—

Discussion Group Questions

1. What is one area of trust building you would like to see in your marriage?
2. What is one area of protection that you think your marriage needs?

CHAPTER 14
A SEVENTY-YEAR VISION & ITS LEGACY

Life with an officer is never dull, predictable, or planned.
Embrace the lifestyle, let go of the little things and
always remember to make time for each other.
MELINA, CALIFORNIA

You know that look old married people give each
other? How they communicate with their eyes from
across the room? It's not because their life was so
happy all the time and easy. It's because they went
through hell, and made it through together.
CHIEF BRENT NEWMAN

Being a cop's wife is tough. The title of this book explores the dichotomy of being a law enforcement spouse. On one hand, I must be strong—stubborn even, in the pursuit of a lasting law enforcement marriage. But at the same time, he leans on me—looks to me for support. I'm his backup at home. I represent strength, yet gentleness.

We must fight for our marriages because of the nature of our husbands' jobs, yet we are careful to choose attitudes that soothe, encourage, and strengthen. We are advocates for our husbands, and there is no sitting on the sidelines. The life we chose with our officers is one that is lived out with character. We are tenacious fighters and gentle lovers.

As you process all that you've read within the pages of this book, I ask one final question. What is the vision for your marriage? What do you want your marriage to look like years from now? If you meander aimlessly from one year to the next, you'll get just that—time gone by that you can't account for. But if you want to have a marriage that is meaningful, you must take proactive steps toward that goal.

A Vision of Marriage

Back in chapter one, I described the Hooker Oak Tree in Chico that was found to be two trees that grew together over time. I witnessed a marriage like this just a few miles from that old Hooker Oak. In February 2011, my grandparents celebrated their seventieth wedding anniversary. I love the old pictures of their young faces, polished and smiling, my grandma in her elegant 40's-style gown and my grandfather in his suit. They've been through the Depression, World War II, the Korean War, the Vietnam War, the Hippie Generation, the Cold War, the Kennedy Assassination, Martin Luther King, 9/11, the War on Terror, and the electronic revolution, among many other world events. Personally, they went through military deployment during wartime, several other careers, their son almost dying of a heart attack, the deaths of their parents, siblings and many friends, several homes in three states, weddings of descendants, divorces of descendants, serious health issues, sending grandchildren to war, and more good memories than they can recount. They had three children, nine grandchildren, four step-grandchildren, twenty-five great-grandchildren, one step-great-grandchild, and one great-great-grandchild at that time. My grandpa said, "It's a little scary to see what all we've created!"

I asked my grandparents, "What's your secret? How have you stayed married all these years?"

My grandpa chuckled a bit and then said, "That's simple. God and a love between us." As the three of us talked, they elaborated a bit more, finishing each other's sentences like they did for many years. "When two people get married, you become one. When you're one, you have to stick together, or it doesn't work out! We also have had a lot of support from family, first from our parents, and now from you guys. We learned a lot of things over the years, and we tried to never make the same mistake twice. It's been a lot of little things that have all worked together."

Commitment. Flexibility. Communication. Mutual respect. Strong foundation. Support system. Perseverance. Trust. A lot of little things can work towards keeping a couple together—the same things I've written about in this book. But it isn't about just staying together—it's about building a good life together. One that defies statistics and thrives in the midst of difficulties.

My grandparents were married for almost 73 years. They were inseparable for most of that time, raising four generations before they both passed in 2014. The final separation was painful, yet peaceful. My grandma held my grandpa's hand, sang a hymn in his ear, and gave him permission to go.

Not only did they live a legacy of love and faithfulness amidst really trying circumstances over the years, they both demonstrated the ultimate act of loyalty at the end—Grandpa hanging on because he didn't want to leave his lifelong love, and Grandma releasing him because of his pain and suffering. What a beautiful way to end a life well lived.

As a testimony to the legacy of marriage, I now wear my grandmother's last wedding ring with the ring Brent gave me on our wedding day. It represents over 100 years of marriage!

My parents have followed in their footsteps—they've been married 53 years at the time of this writing, and they are each other's best friends. Their lives together represent a loving home, a safe place for kindness that their community, children, grandchildren, and extended family to enjoy. Brent and I are another generation behind them, celebrating over 29 years at the time of this publishing. We are blessed to carry on this legacy.

It is possible to build a great law enforcement marriage. But this takes knowing what you want your marriage to be and then working at it day to day, year to year.

Like my grandparents and parents, Brent and I look forward to growing old together. We want to love each other more deeply than we do today. We have been raising our kids to maturity in a safe and loving home, so that they, too, will raise great kids. It is this vision that spurs us on year after year.

I've talked a lot about different seasons throughout this book. At the time of this writing, Brent and I are on the brink of a new season. Our children are heading off into the world on their own. As Brent's career counts down rapidly towards retirement, we adapt and change as the career changes. As for me, the journey of author, speaker, and nonprofit president promises to allow me to continue building into law enforcement marriages and advocating for the Blue Line Family until I am too old to travel! I love what I do because I love police families.

At some point, Brent's career as a highway patrolman will come to an end. We will have a collection of awesome memories as we begin yet another season in our lives together, just the two of us. In the meantime, we'll keep at it, implementing what I've written on the pages of this book, and reinterpreting the principles to fit the circumstances we face year to year.

Marriage is hard for everyone. Marriage can be even harder for law enforcement. But you and your husband are a special and unique couple because you have willingly served the people in your jurisdiction and have pledged your best effort. You are noble and courageous. My hope and prayer for you both is that you will thrive through the seasons of your marriage in spite of the difficulties, perhaps one day celebrating over seventy awesome years together.

Discussion Group Questions

1. Identify an older married couple that you know who've done marriage well. What is one character trait you see in their relationship?
2. What season are you in right now? How is that affecting your marriage?
3. What is your vision for your marriage? Be specific.
4. Put together a group date night with your husbands to celebrate your marriages.

If you liked *A CHiP on my Shoulder*, consider
A Marriage in Progress:
Tactical Support for Law Enforcement Relationships.
It is the companion book for officers!

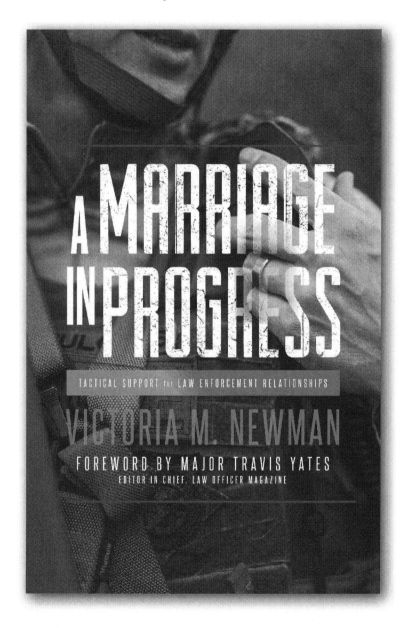

ABOUT THE AUTHOR

Victoria M. Newman has been a cop wife for almost 30 years. Her husband, Brent, is a Chief with the California Highway Patrol. They have lived in many areas of California, starting with the Los Angeles area and currently serving Northern California from the Sacramento area. They have four children, and one grandchild.

Victoria is Founder and President of How2LoveYourCop, a charitable organization that strives to help police families thrive relationally, emotionally, and spiritually. She has partnered with departments, wives' groups, ministries, chaplaincies, organizations, foundations, and individuals to bring about the best possible resources for those in law enforcement.

She has written two books for law enforcement families, three other books as a ghostwriter, and has consulted with at least a dozen other authors on their published works. She is a sought-after speaker for law enforcement and military audiences, trained as a law enforcement chaplain and peer support member, and mentors several police spouses and couples (with her husband). She is also a columnist for LawOfficer magazine.

Victoria is a woman of deep faith in Jesus Christ, and has attended and served at Bayside Church of Granite Bay for almost 15 years. She taught herself how to cook as a newlywed, homeschooled her children for 10 years (a labor of love), taught Bible studies for over two decades, and has walked through PTSD with loved ones. She is a Chicago Cubs fan (even before it was cool), a baseball mom, and loves to work out at her local gym.

You can reach Victoria at victoria@how2loveyourcop.com.

ABOUT HOW2LOVEYOURCOP

After the release of A CHiP on my Shoulder in 2011, I started hearing from police spouses all over the United States. Soon thereafter, I heard from officers, and then departments. Soon I was flying to places I'd never been to speak to people I'd never met. I started blogging, and Facebook became my new friend.

That is when How2LoveYourCop became a "thing"—I called it an operation that created resources for police families, adding content regularly to my blog, Facebook page, articles, books, a seminar, and speaking engagements.

End of 2016 I began to rethink things in the midst of some really hard days. I realized it was either time to shut it down, or bring on more people—I chose the second option. On Saint Patrick's Day 2017, How2LoveYourCop (H2LYC) became an official corporation, pending tax-exemption status.

At the same time, another organization I had partnered with had made the decision to dissolve. A key person in that organization asked if she could join their marriage and family programs with H2LYC. It was a perfect fit, so I agreed.

H2LYC is now made of two divisions—one that serves the families of active duty officers, and another that serves families that have an officer significantly wounded in the line of duty. Our organization exists to help police families in both divisions thrive relationally, emotionally, and spiritually.

With the expansion of H2LYC, we offer the books, blog, social media content, seminars and speaking engagements from before, but we will add the following:

- Conferences and Retreats for Spouses, Couples, Wounded Officers, and more
- More Law Enforcement Books from Victoria and others
- Information Packets for New Officers, Wounded Officers, Critical Incident Follow-Up, and more
- More partnerships with other organizations to create the best available resources
- Top Notch Videos
- Bible Studies
- Small Group Training
- Family Support & Resources for Critical Incidents, PTSD, and other challenges

H2LYC is run by volunteers who have served in law enforcement or as family members of law enforcement. Several have been through difficult challenges that have given them tried and true insight. If you would like more information, access to other resources, or to offer a donation, please visit our website, www.how2loveyourcop.com.

Made in the USA
Lexington, KY
13 September 2019